Mojisola Adebayo is a playwright, performer, director, producer, workshop facilitator and lecturer. She has a BA in Drama and Theatre Arts, an MA in Physical Theatre and her PhD is entitled *Afriquia Theatre: Creating Black Queer Ubuntu Through Performance* (Goldsmiths, Royal Holloway and Queen Mary, University of London). Mojisola trained extensively with Augusto Boal and is an international specialist in Theatre of the Oppressed, often working in locations of crisis and conflict. She has worked in theatre, radio and television, on four continents, over the past twenty-five years, performing in over fifty productions, writing, devising and directing over thirty plays, and leading countless workshops, from Antarctica to Zimbabwe. Her own authored plays include *Moj of the Antarctic: An African Odyssey* (Lyric Hammersmith and Ovalhouse, London), *Muhammad Ali and Me* (Ovalhouse, Albany Theatre, London and UK touring), *48 Minutes for Palestine* (Ashtar Theatre and international touring), *Desert Boy* (Albany Theatre, London and UK touring), *The Listeners* (Pegasus Theatre, Oxford), *I Stand Corrected* (Artscape, Ovalhouse, London and international touring) and *The Interrogation of Sandra Bland* (Bush Theatre, London). Her publications include *Mojisola Adebayo: Plays One* (Oberon Books), *48 Minutes for Palestine* in *Theatre in Pieces* (Methuen), *The Interrogation of Sandra Bland* in *Black Lives, Black Words* (Oberon Books), *The Theatre for Development Handbook* (Pan, co-written with John Martin and Manisha Mehta) as well as academic chapters published by Methuen, Palgrave Macmillan and various journals. Mojisola Adebayo is a Fellow of the Royal Society of Literature; an Associate Artist with Pan Arts, Building the Anti-Racist Classroom Collective and Black Lives, Black Words; an Honorary Fellow of Rose Bruford College, a Visiting Lecturer at Goldsmiths and a Lecturer at Queen Mary, University of London. She has recently been awarded a Fellowship at Potsdam University (Germany). Her play *Wind/Rush Generation(s)*, commissioned by the National Theatre (Connections), opens in 2020. STA~~ ~~ 2021. See **www.mojisolaadebayo.c**

T0347913

Mojisola Adebayo

PLAYS TWO

I Stand Corrected
Asara and the Sea-Monstress
Oranges and Stones
The Interrogation of Sandra Bland
STARS

OBERON BOOKS
LONDON

WWW.OBERONBOOKS.COM

First published in 2019 by Oberon Books Ltd
521 Caledonian Road, London N7 9RH
Tel: +44 (0) 20 7607 3637 / Fax: +44 (0) 20 7607 3629
e-mail: info@oberonbooks.com
www.oberonbooks.com

PB ISBN: 9781786828002
E ISBN: 9781786828019

Cover illustration © Candice Purwin

eBook conversion by Lapiz Digital Services, India.

10 9 8 7 6 5 4 3 2 1

For Nicole

Contents

Acknowledgements

I hereby extend a huge thank you to Debo Adebayo, Mamela
Nyamza, Edward Muallem, Rajha Shakiry and all of the
artists and creative contributors whose individual names are
too many to repeat here but who are duly acknowledged
at the start of each play. These productions were only
made possible through your extraordinary creativity and
commitment. Thanks to each and every one of you. There
are other people who have supported the writing and making
of these plays whom I would now like to take a moment
to thank. Thank you to my Editor, Serena Grasso and also
James Hogan and everyone at Oberon Books. You have
changed the face of theatre publishing in Britain. Thank
you to Professor Lynette Goddard for your introduction and
support, and Candice Purwin for your beautiful artwork on
the cover. Thank you to all of the individuals that enabled
the development of these works, especially Shante Needham
and all of Sandra Bland's family. Thank you to all of the
workers at the theatre companies, venues and organisations
that enabled the development of these works, especially: Jean
September of British Council Cape Town, Suha Khuffash
of British Council Palestine, Marlene LeRoux of Artscape,
Rachel Anderson and Cis O'Boyle of idle women, Simeilia
Hodge-Dallaway of Artistic Directors of the Future (ADF)
and Elayce Ismail through ADF, Reginald Edmund of Black

Lives, Black Words, Madani Younis and Omar Elerian of Bush Theatre, Stella Kanu and Owen Calvert-Lyons of Ovalhouse, Edward Muallem, Iman Auon, Fida Jiris and all the team at Ashtar Theatre, Raidene Carter and Gavin Barlow of Albany Theatre, Rosamunde Hutt and Carl Miller of Unicorn Theatre, Caroline Jester of Birmingham REP and Isabel Waidner of Dostoyevsky Wannabe. Thank you also to Andrew Ellerby and Deborah Williams of Arts Council England. Thank you to our funders Arts Council England, Unity Theatre Trust, British Council Cape Town, British Council Palestine and Queen Mary University of London, Centre for Public Engagement. Thank you to my colleagues at Queen Mary, University of London (QMUL) for the PhD scholarship that enabled two of these works. Thank you to my Primary PhD Supervisor in the Drama Department at QMUL, Dr Catherine Silverstone. Thank you to my Secondary Supervisor Professor Caoimhe McAvinchey, as well as Dr Nadia Davids and Professor Lois Weaver. I am grateful to all of my comrades in the Department of Theatre and Performance at Goldsmiths, University of London especially my respective Heads of Department whilst I wrote these plays, Professor Anna Furse and Professor Osita Okagbue. Blessings and appreciation to everyone who bought tickets for these plays, contributed freely to post-show discussions, workshops and the community chorus. Thank you to the children who gave feedback on *Asara*, especially Barney and Arthur, Alice and Emily, Thomas and James, and all the grown-up 'Marys' too. I want to take this opportunity to extend my deep gratitude to the family of friends who carried me through periods of illness and injury whilst writing these plays, including: Sandra Vacciana, Franc Ashman, Jeff Banks, Anna Wallbank, Kay Soord, Stella Barnes, Nicky Bashall, Paul Woodward, Anna Napier, Nadia Davids, Jean September, Del LaGrace Volcano, Claudine Rousseau, Ali Pottinger, Rita Das, Charlie Folorunsho, Antonia Kemi Coker, Katy Forkha, Alison Halstead, Ellie Beedham, Rajha Shakiry, Tariq Alvi, Bid Mosaku, Jacqui Beckford, John Martin, Debora Mina, Mita

Banerjee, Catherine Silverstone, Sue Mayo, Manisha Mehta, Jules Hussey, Sue Giovanni, Cathy Tyson, Jilna Shah, S. Ama Wray, Elizabeth da Rosa, Carole Jones, Hilary Marshall, Alisa Lebow, Başak Ertür, Nanna Heidenreich, Fine Freiburg, Sadhvi Dar, Deni Francis, Crin Claxton, Luca Claxton-Francis, Leni Goddard, Semsem Kuherhi, Sarah Ives, Nesta Jones, Steven Dykes, Styler and Jahni Tafari, Avaes Mohammad and so many more. I would not have made it without your support. Thank you Elyse Dodgson, rest in peace dear heart, your legacy continues. Thank you dear Giuseppe, my guardian angel. Huge thanks to my beloved kin, especially my brother Debo Adebayo, my mother Anne Marie Adebayo, as well as Klaus Zimmermann, Louise Hennessey, Remi Adebayo, Tomisin Adebayo, Dotun, Yinka, Folarin, Diran, Tayo, Tunde, Funmilayo and Funmilola Adebayo and all of my beautiful inspirational cousins (too many to mention) – ubuntu. Last but not least, Nicole Wolf, Liebe meines Lebens, thank you for everything. 'Me, We' – Muhammad Ali.

Introduction

February 2019. Britain is in a state of turmoil as the government negotiates the deal to leave the European Union following the 2016 EU Referendum. The clock is ticking down towards the planned leave date of 29 March 2019 and the precise terms of the Brexit deal (or no deal) are yet to be agreed as talks falter on the question of the Irish border. Meanwhile, the USA's forty-fifth president Donald Trump continues to make the news headlines after he shut down his government when Congress voted against funding the construction of a Mexican border wall. The very idea of borders raises questions about rights, movement and power, about who is allowed to or prevented from crossing and about how borders are maintained and policed. The Windrush scandal rumbles on, as long-established British residents are shaken by questions about their right to remain living in the UK and new revelations about wrongful deportations continue to emerge. Recently released figures suggest a 54% increase in the number of teenagers going to hospital with stab wounds, and there are almost daily reports of stabbing and shooting fatalities, new families thrown into turmoil by sudden loss.

Within such a troubled political climate, social media and hashtag activist campaigns such as #BlackLivesMatter and #MeToo continue to demand fair and equal rights for Black, Queer, Women's and Transgender* lives. We are making the most of a right to respond to current affairs and problematic political rhetoric, and we seem to be becoming more able to open up discussions about difficult and sensitive issues, helped by the advent of social media and the use of smartphone technologies. Bystanders become witnesses and material recorded locally on hand-held devices makes it onto global news agendas. A number of recently published books also openly tackle the difficulties of talking about race, confronting and challenging white fragility and white privilege. Theatre, too, plays its role in representing resistant voices in times of crisis and instability. Many practitioners continue to use theatre to raise consciences and provocatively shake audiences from the comforts of privileged individual existences.

Questions can be asked about the most effective forms of activist theatre, about which forms of theatre might best enable a provocation on these urgent social concerns, about the role that activist practitioners play in a period of heightened conservatism in public and political life, and about how contemporary practitioners are carving out spaces in which to link art and activism. Some answers to these questions are found in Mojisola Adebayo's recent works, which bridge gaps between art and activism, community and professional theatre, blackness, disability and queerness. Mojisola's performances have been presented and debated in theatres and festivals, academic conferences and political meetings worldwide – Austria, Brazil, Britain, China, Germany, Ghana, Ireland, Jordan, Norway, Palestine/Israel, Poland, Russia, Singapore, Spain, South Africa, Sweden and the USA. These five plays represent the diverse scope and content of Mojisola's work and demonstrate an ongoing commitment to an artistic practice that is both stylistically innovative and politically astute. From plays for children and young audiences, to international work in Palestine and South Africa and collaborations with sign language interpreters and other practitioners, these plays share the experimental forms and a commitment to making audiences reflect on the important issues that are the heart of Mojisola's creative practice.

Having recently completed a PhD about Afriquia theatre, Mojisola's interest in Black Queer experiences of gender, sexuality and human rights remains paramount in her recent theatrical work. *I Stand Corrected* is a drama and dance notated text that confronts the issue of so-called 'corrective rape' of lesbians and trans* men in South Africa alongside the equal marriage debate in Britain. The play premiered in Cape Town, followed by a run at London's Ovalhouse Theatre in 2012. The production was developed as a collaboration between Mojisola and South African dancer and choreographer Mamela Nyamza, utilising and blending their distinctive performance strengths and approaches. Using the format of a wedding that goes wrong, their physical, visual and poetically spoken and sung exploration moves fluidly between dance, movement and words spoken directly to the audience. In a community church hall Charlie, a lesbian bride, waits impatiently for her girlfriend to arrive for their marriage. The audience are involved in the production, positioned as the wedding guests, who anticipate the arrival alongside Charlie, wondering what the explanation could be for her fiancée's lateness. At the same time, in an alleyway in South Africa, Zodwa recites township names as she wriggles herself free from the dustbin in which she is squashed in a half-dressed state. *I Stand Corrected* is an intimate, tender, and humorous exploration of gender performativity, marriage rights, and the mistreatment of Black lesbians in South Africa.

As well as dealing with important themes, Mojisola's creations remain attentive to the entire experience of being in a theatre, striving to ensure that her plays are inclusive and accessible for all audiences. Her collaborations with British Sign Language interpreter Jacqui Beckford work towards a fully integrated approach where the words and the movement form one language, with Beckford performing alongside Mojisola as both character and BSL interpreter simultaneously. The integration of British Sign Language is imperative to the accessibility of *Asara and the Sea-Monstress*, originally developed as part of the Emerge Writers Attachment to the Birmingham

Repertory Theatre and the Unicorn Theatre, and playing at the Albany in London. *Asara and the Sea-Monstress* is a play for primary school-aged children, which addresses homophobia through West African storytelling. As a piece designed for children to explore the idea of difference and homophobia, the story is told through the metaphor of the experiences of a left-handed girl living in a right-handed world. Mojisola's fluid writing and performance style is maximised through the merging of the many influences that she draws from and responds to in her poetic storytelling.

Oranges and Stones is made through a collaborative devising process between Mojisola Adebayo and Ashtar Theatre, whose creative output combines aesthetic arts in a bid to raise cultural awareness about lives in Palestine. A play without words (with audio-description for blind audience members where requested), scripted in stage directions and music, *Oranges and Stones* evocatively illustrates the occupation of Palestine as a two-hander about a man who enters a woman's home with his suitcase, places it on the floor and refuses to leave. Although particular to the occupation of Palestine, there are also contemporary resonances with debates about immigration, about who has the right to move, and about those who use their sense of power and entitlement to colonise others.

The Interrogation of Sandra Bland is a verbatim transcript of the roadside arrest of Sandra Bland that led to her premature death in police custody in 2015. The arrest is transcribed word-for-word from the dash cam of the police car that pulled her over and crafted to be performed by a chorus of one hundred Black women. The collective voices of the Black women's chorus rise together to match the shouting of the white male police officer, in resistance to and defiance of the long history of institutional racism and sexism that manifests itself in the way the police treat Black people. Incidents where Black lives are lost during or soon after being in contact with the police are shared through social media posts and tweets, and captured in films such as *Fruitvale Station* (2014) or *The Hate U Give* (2018), leading to wider public knowledge. Mojisola's transcript of the arrest of Sandra Bland is a powerful use of verbatim technique, modelled to maximise the emotional and testimonial power of the piece. The rehearsal draft published here shows how the chorus can work in performance with the scope to make different decisions within one's own directorial journey. At the Bush Theatre, where *The Interrogation of Sandra Bland* premiered as part of the *Black Lives, Black Words* project in March 2017, the show was performed on a smaller scale than intended, with a chorus of about thirty Black women, and yet the effect was still powerful. In April 2019, the piece was performed again as the culmination of a three-day *Black Lives, Black Words* festival at the Goodman Theatre, Chicago, that was 'dedicated to culturally diverse women and female-identified artists, leaders and activists.' As a theatrical response to the #BlackLivesMatter and #SayHerName movements, *The Interrogation of Sandra Bland* is a short play with a large affective impact, the echoes of which have remained with me long after leaving the auditorium.

STARS is Mojisola's latest play, so far seen in a rehearsed reading at the Ovalhouse Theatre in spring 2018 and slated for a full production in 2019. Centering on an elderly woman who goes on an intergalactic space adventure in search of her first orgasm, the show is performed by two actors who play Mrs and all of the other characters with whom she interacts. The narrative is underscored with projected animation and a soundscape of ambient house and space-themed music mixed live on stage by Mojisola's DJ brother Debo. *STARS* is a rich and ambitious piece that intersects themes of sexuality and sexual desire in ageing women with concerns about Female Genital Mutilation and the non-consensual medical interventions made on intersex bodies. While these terms are not explicitly named in the text, they are an urgent backdrop to the main narrative through-line: an exhortation to radical acceptance in life and love.

Mojisola's plays grapple with racial and sexual identities and our experiences of who we are and how we understand ourselves in relation to the wider world. The plays collected in this anthology are also evocative of twenty-first century Black British theatre's engagement with wider concerns, its move beyond identity politics to open up discussions about the big social and political issues that affect and determine our lives. Through these sensitive explorations of Black LGBTQI* experiences at the intersection of the personal and the political and the local and the global, Mojisola's performances create spaces for increased understanding, empathy and action.

Lynette Goddard
Professor in Black Theatre and Performance,
Royal Holloway, University of London

I STAND CORRECTED

Dedicated to all survivors and victims of
(so-called 'corrective') homophobic and
transphobic hate rape

I Stand Corrected was commissioned by Artscape Women's Festival (Cape Town, South Africa). It was first performed on 7 August 2012 in the Arena Theatre, Artscape and toured to London, Singapore and Soweto with the following creative team:

Creative Team

PRODUCERS MOJISOLA ADEBAYO AND MARLENE LE ROUX OF ARTSCAPE

CO-CREATOR / CO-DIRECTOR / CO-PERFORMER PLAYING CHARLIE MOJISOLA ADEBAYO

CO-CREATOR / CO-DIRECTOR / CO-PERFORMER PLAYING ZODWA MAMELA NYAMZA

WRITER MOJISOLA ADEBAYO

CHOREOGRAPHER MAMELA NYAMZA

SET AND COSTUME DESIGNER RAJHA SHAKIRY

LIGHTING DESIGNER MANNIE MANIM

MUSIC SUPERVISOR DEBO ADEBAYO OF MIX 'N' SYNC

STAGE MANAGER (SOUTH AFRICA AND SINGAPORE) JEROME CHAPMAN

PRODUCTION MANAGER (SOUTH AFRICA AND SINGAPORE) ALFRED REITMANN

PRODUCTION AND STAGE MANAGER (LONDON) CRIN CLAXTON

CURATOR OF PHOTOGRAPHY (TOURING WITH THE SHOW) / CAPE TOWN LESBIAN COMMUNITY FACILITATOR / POSTER IMAGE ARTIST ZANELE MUHOLI

BLACK LESBIAN/TRANS COMMUNITY DEVELOPMENT WORKSHOP PARTICIPANTS AND PROTEST SINGERS OYAMA, SISIPHO, PHUMEZA, SIPHOKAZI, LINDEKA, GCOBISA, CHRISTIE, YEWLISA, HBMELA, PATHO, NZULA, PEARL, TERRA, NAMHLA (AND OTHERS)

VIDEO DOCUMENTATION SHELLEY BARRY (CAPE TOWN), SUE GIOVANNI (LONDON)

ADMINISTRATION DEBBIE DELON (CAPE TOWN)

Note on the text

This is a performance script/score consisting of stage directions, movement/dance notation, speech and song lyrics. Italics are used to denote stage action, directions and sung lyrics. The scenes are separated out here to aid a sense of narrative, but many scenes actually cross over each other or run concurrently. There should be a seamless flow from one moment to the next.

Characters

ZODWA NDLOVU, a black lesbian woman from a Cape Town township, a graduate lighting technician, in her early thirties. She is dead but at the start she does not know this. Her spirit, however, is very much alive.

CHARLIE BROWNING, Zodwa's partner. She is a middle-class, mixed-heritage/black, lesbian, girls' cricket coach, on a trip from England, in her late thirties.

Setting

An urban black African township in South Africa. The present. An alleyway, a shack, and a church hall decorated for a wedding. The three locations are all merged through one set that is abstract in design. No set changes.

PRESET

Pre-show music and a dimly lit stage as the audience enter. There is haze in the auditorium, as if a fire has been smoking and dying.

The set is reminiscent of the back wall of a South African township alleyway, created from burnt horizontal wooden slats. The wall opens out at a forty-five degree angle on stage left side. The alleyway is merged with an informal community church hall used for parties and functions decorated with balloons and a township shack. A steel fire bin used for fires and a large steel oil drum are set close to the angled wall, mid-stage left. An aluminium rubbish bin that will be 'ZODWA's bin' is empty in preset, slightly downstage of the other objects.

There are three black plastic bags full of rubbish around the bins. One of the bags contains old CDs, a half-eaten satsuma, an empty tub of yoghurt, a nearly empty bottle of vodka (containing a small amount of water), a very old discarded radio, plus various 'women's items' including a broken pair of sunglasses, one high-heeled shoe, an opened unused slim-fit tampon, old stockings, red lipstick, a used women's condom, some face wipes and a Shape *magazine (April 2012).*

The floor is black (dance floor for movement purposes), but there is a strip of white running the upstage width of the stage onto which there is ash. This might be painted to look like ash or be theatrical ash. The white strip is reminiscent of a pathway for a bride in a church but is ashen, thus merged with the burnt alleyway feel.

In this area, a huge white skirt, the bottom half of a wedding dress and a jacket float from a huge bunch of helium white wedding balloons close to the wall. The dress may actually need to be attached to the back wall, but it must look as if it is floating from the balloons. The image almost looks like an angel floating below clouds.

A light bulb hangs mid-stage left. This area denotes ZODWA's shack.

SCENE – PROTEST AND RAIN

We hear the sound of women singing a lesbian protest song (To the tune of an old anti-apartheid protest song) in Xhosa, outside a courthouse. The words are translated as:
'It's bad, bad, bad,
But even if they rape us
Even if they kill us
We shall go on
Being us'

The singing is drowned out by the sound of rain on corrugated iron roofs.

The preset state fades to black.

A flash of lightning through which we can just see the bins against the back wall.

In the darkness, the performer playing ZODWA takes up her position. Her legs, arms and face are smeared in charcoal.

Flash of lightning. We now see ZODWA's upturned dead body in the empty bin and her legs sticking up, frozen still, with tight boxer shorts on and bare feet.

Black. Sound of rain continues.

Flash of light. As well as ZODWA stuck in the bin, we also see CHARLIE upstage right, on the white strip of the floor, jumping up and down, shaking out her body of nerves. She wears white slacks and the top half of a wedding dress.

Flash of light. CHARLIE is gone and ZODWA is kicking her legs vigorously, as if the soles of her feet are being touched by something extremely hot.

Black.

In the darkness, ZODWA moves to her third position, lying in the bin on its side.

Rain stops slowly.

SCENE – WOZA ZODWA (ZODWA RISE UP)

Gradual sunrise over the stage during the scene.

Still inside the bin, ZODWA pushes herself with her feet away from the wall, with some difficulty. ZODWA is trying to figure out how to move.

She rolls slightly then figures out how to sit up. Her legs face downstage. The bin is still over her head. It comes to her waist.

ZODWA's legs are confused and they get twisted up. Eventually ZODWA pulls her legs wide apart, almost in splits, still on the floor with the bin on her head.

She flexes her feet.

Then she figures out how to shuffle on her bottom with her legs wide apart and she moves downstage with some speed, flexing and pointing her feet.

Now ZODWA wants to get up. First she sits like a frog, with her knees turned in on the floor.

Then ZODWA flips her knees up and places her feet flat on the ground. She pushes up to sit in a low squat.

She rises up and down in the squat.

Eventually ZODWA figures out how to get from squatting to standing.

ZODWA brings her thighs and feet together tightly. She shuffles around with her feet in parallel. It is difficult to get anywhere.

Then she spreads her legs outwards and moves in demi-plié, downstage.

Then her arms suddenly emerge from the bin.

Her hands, like her legs, are confused at first. The fingers get tangled up. Eventually she figures out how to express with her hands. Gestures are coming back to her.

With gestures she moves from downstage left to right, gesturing to the audience, trying to figure out how to communicate.

ZODWA begins to lean her torso backwards in the bin while moving left to right, and discovers that she can now sense people out there watching her. Her gesturing hands signal accusations/questions that convey the meaning 'was it you?' She also repeats the word 'you in hushed tones.

Downstage right, ZODWA's gestures become pointing fingers. The pointing finger of her right hand starts to wag faster and faster like a flaccid penis.

Gripped by a memory she does not yet understand, ZODWA starts to back away from the audience, further upstage, conveying a sense of fear. She turns around trying to see behind her, though the bin is still on her head and she can see nothing. It looks quite absurd.

Her fear/memory of fear makes her want to run. She starts running very fast on the spot, turning until her back is to the audience.

She begins to lift the bin over her head and starts to run randomly around the space in a state of fear.

She runs towards the wall at speed and discovers she cannot get beyond it.

She moves along the wall from stage left and then slides down it.

From a very low position, she starts to walk, crouching, along the wall, left to right.

She eventually tires from this and starts to bend forward until the bin lands on the floor.

Still inside the bin, ZODWA's arms emerge.

She turns herself to the side and we see her hands starting to look as if they are praying or begging for mercy.

She then returns her arms inside the bin and starts to beat it, as if she is trapped and trying to get out.

This builds until she eventually flips her head out of the bin.

ZODWA gasps for air like a fish out of water.

We now see that she is wearing a sweat-top with arms cut off near the top. She also has a technicians light on a piece of elastic around her neck.

She then holds the edge of the bin and puts her whole body weight onto it, her arms shaking, as if she is going to be sick inside the bin.

She then turns to hide behind the bin and begins to move it downstage, away from the wall. It looks as though the bin is moving on its own.

She folds her hands around the bin and hugs it, as one might do to a lover.

She then places her hands at the top of the bin and pops her eyes over the top. She seems fearful.

She starts to push the bin, using her head, moving towards the rubbish bags.

She slowly moves away from the bin, looking more closely at the rubbish bags now.

Slowly she gets to standing and tentatively moves towards the rubbish bags.

She kicks a bag, as if to check whether it is alive.

On tip-toes, she moves around the second bag.

She then pulls open 'her' black rubbish bag (containing the items listed above).

ZODWA puts her whole body inside the black bag and rummages around.

She turns on the radio inside it, which startles her.

She pulls the radio out and finds a station where the music moves her.

Her eyes begin to 'dance'.

The confused eye dance moves through ZODWA's body from her head to her shoulders, chest and legs in a kind of crumping style that is all her own.

After some dancing she begins to explore the other objects in the black bag.

ZODWA finds an old CD. She puts it to her eye and looks through the centre hole. She uses the CD like a monocle to help her look around at the other objects. She sees a discarded copy of Shape *magazine (dated April 2012).*

ZODWA turns her aluminium bin over, making a table surface to place the magazine down on. She flicks through the magazine, playfully impersonating each stereotypical image of femininity that she sees, thus 'learning' how to be a 'correct' woman.

ZODWA works through imitating various poses in several positions around and over the bin. It is quite comical.

Eventually she returns to the image she is drawn to most (though she does not know why). It is the image of a butch male. She impersonates this picture.

ZODWA then rolls up the magazine and turns off the radio. She needs to have a shit.

She takes her aluminium bin away from the other objects to find a 'private' space.

She turns the bin over, making it into a toilet. She pulls down her boxer shorts and sits on it, as if to shit, whilst casually flicking through the magazine, facing stage right.

She adjusts her light to around her head, like a miner. It enables her to read in the dim light.

SCENE – WEDDING MARCH

A change in lighting state from the alleyway to the church hall. The audience are effectively the wedding guests and will be referred to as such throughout. Even their show programmes are configured as an order of service. There needs to be some house light on the audience during the wedding speeches.

Music – 'We Have All the Time in the World' by Louis Armstrong.

Upstage stage left, CHARLIE enters in an extremely slow walk; it is a stylised wedding march. She wears white silk slacks – the bottom half of a suit – and heels. On top she wears the top half of a wedding dress, a white bust. Her head is wrapped with white cloth in an African style. She has jewellery. Her costume has hints of traditional Xhosa South African style. She holds a bouquet of wedding flowers. She is full of joy, trying to control her breathing and emotions.

CHARLIE travels slowly along the white path upstage, turning a corner at upstage left where the wall angles. She walks straight downstage left, where she stops at the imaginary 'altar'.

Music fades down as she arrives.

CHARLIE waits politely at the 'altar' with flowers in her hands. She smiles and nods lightly at individual guests in the church/the audience.

CHARLIE waits and continues to wait during the next scene.

SCENE – ZODWA'S ZODIAC

Still sitting/shitting, ZODWA starts to read the astrology section of the magazine. She is slowly remembering how to read and how to speak. She is trying figure out who she is or was and who she is now supposed to be and trying to learn how to be a 'corrected' woman.

ZODWA: *(Scanning months of the year listed in the magazine.)*
January. February. March. April. May. June. July. August.
September… *(Recognizing this month as her birth month.)*
September. September… *(Trying to remember her birthday.)*
22nd. 1976. Virgo. The virgin. *(Reading aloud from the magazine, ZODWA is figuring out the language she is reading, which is both familiar and somehow foreign. Her voice is almost robotic.)* 'There's something delightfully feminine about Miss Virgo even when she's wearing tomboy clothes and having a bad hair day. Slim, pretty with natural grace

31

and big, wide open eyes, Miss Virgo was born under the sign of the celestial maiden so she just can't help being gorgeous[1].'

SCENE – CHARLIE WAITS

This scene crosses over in time with the scene above.

CHARLIE looks behind her, as if to see if her partner is coming.

CHARLIE mouths 'what time is it?' to an audience member. An audience member might tell her the time.

CHARLIE waits.

CHARLIE mouths 'what time is it now?'

An audience member might reply.

CHARLIE waits. Smells the flowers. Smiles. Waits. Gets bored. Uncomfortable. Embarrassed. Nervous. Anxious. Angry. A rollercoaster of emotions but very repressed. She plays with the petals of the flowers. Shows signs of getting a little upset. Mouths 'sorry, what's the time now?' Gets the answer. Looks up. Starts to get really upset. Laughs at herself slightly, shaking her head.

CHARLIE: I'm gonna kill her. *(A beat.)* I'm gonna fucking kill her.

CHARLIE suddenly gives the flowers to an audience member on the front row, removes her high-heeled shoes, and storms out the way she came in.

As CHARLIE exits, ZODWA very slowly slides down inside the bin, bottom first, until her legs are in the air, her arms are out to the sides, and we can no longer see her head. She looks as though she has been squashed in the bin, still holding the magazine.

---

1   http://www.nowmagazine.co.uk/horoscopes/extra/260896/virgo--your-character – accessed 15 June 2012.

ZODWA rips a page from the magazine and starts to rub it, to soften its texture so she can use it as toilet paper. As she does this she recites names of various black townships:

ZODWA: Langa, Nyanga, Gugulethu, Soweto, Khayelitsha, Orlando East… *(Etc.)*

SCENE – PHONE CALLS

During ZODWA's speech above, CHARLIE comes back on with a mobile phone. She positions herself mid-stage right, as if she has found a quiet corner between the church and the church hall. She mutters.

CHARLIE: Come on come on come on…

There is no reply.

CHARLIE starts to text ZODWA. The sound of her tapping on the mobile phone keys turns into random musical sounds. ZODWA starts to move her free arms to the rhythm of the sounds, making talking gestures. This becomes a gestural dance that continues through CHARLIE's off-stage speech below.

CHARLIE exits sharply again stage right. We can just hear her talking off stage to one of ZODWA's friends. This character can be played by an Assistant Stage Manager backstage who may read their lines. They are barely audible.

CHARLIE: I can't get through.

VOICE: No it's dead.

CHARLIE: Did you go back to the shack?

VOICE: She's not there.

CHARLIE: Are you sure?

VOICE: Of course.

CHARLIE: Well how am I supposed to know?!

VOICE: Calm down.

CHARLIE: I am calm. How about Robyn's bar?

VOICE: You could try.

CHARLIE: What, you expect me to go dressed like this –
I've got a hundred people waiting out there. What if she
turns up?

VOICE: Everyone will understand.

CHARLIE: No, no, I've got to stay – don't you understand
ENGLISH! Sorry. Sorry I'm just… Look I've got to go
and say something, everybody's waiting.

*ZODWA starts to eat the magazine. She is trying to figure out what
her feeling of hunger is. She spits the paper bits through CHARLIE's
action and text below.*

SCENE – CHARLIE STRAIGHTENS THE MIC

*CHARLIE re-enters, carrying a microphone that is bent at angles with
wire in knots around it. CHARLIE places the mic downstage right and
tries to unravel it.*

*During this scene ZODWA starts to feel tired. She pulls herself out of the
bin. Places it back by the rubbish bags and uses it as a pillow to rest on.*

CHARLIE: *(Muttering.)* Bloody thing's bent. *(To the audience.)*
Is it straight? Does it look straight to you? *(Tapping the mic
then speaking into it.)* Can you hear me at the back? Hi
everyone. Thanks very much for coming. As you can see
there's been a slight…hitch. *(On the word 'hitch' CHARLIE
gets upset again. Composing herself, CHARLIE returns to the
mic.)* Sorry. Look, Zodwa's not at home and she's not with
any of her friends, obviously, because you're all here.
(Uncomfortable laughter from CHARLIE.) There's probably a
perfectly reasonable explanation so we're just gonna give

it a little bit more time. If that's okay? *(CHARLIE wanders off the mic momentarily.)* Actually has anyone got her mum's phone number just in case she – no you're right. Bad idea. What would I say? 'Kunjani, Mrs Ndlovu. This is Zodwa's *friend.*' Your big fat gay wedding is probably not the best time to come out to your girlfriend's parents. Sorry, you're probably all really hungry by now, there's no point wasting all the food, so grab some, finger food *(CHARLIE gets a plate of food and a bowl of fruit from offstage whilst talking, then hands it to audiences members to pass around)*, some fruit or whatever *(CHARLIE takes a red apple from the fruit bowl, throws and catches it and places it in her pocket, as if it were a cricket ball)*, and um how about some music. *(CHARLIE gestures to the DJ in the sound box.)*

Music plays. It comes in at the chorus of 'Hello' by Lionel Ritchie.

ZODWA wakes up from her short deep sleep.

CHARLIE takes in the music for a moment and then…

CHARLIE: Perhaps not that one. No, no, not that one. Can we have something more upbeat?

DJ plays 'Baby Come Back' by UB40, bringing it in at the chorus.

ZODWA starts to rummage through the rubbish bin. Looking for something to eat and drink. She eats the half-eaten satsuma and drinks from the vodka bottle.

CHARLIE: *(Irritated.)* Can we have something else, something a bit more… African.

DJ plays 'Beloved' by Tandile Mandela.

CHARLIE: That'll do.

The track gets faster and faster during the scene. The track also plays backwards at points and is warped.

CHARLIE exits, putting on her shoes as she goes out, stage left.

ZODWA comes out of the bin and starts exploring the rubbish again.

SCENE – WHAT KIND OF WOMAN?

Music continues from the scene above.

ZODWA starts using the rubbish to make herself into an ideal 'corrected' woman. She cleans her face with the wipes, using the CD as a mirror. She puts lipstick over her face, puts a stocking on her head, followed by the yoghurt tub. Puts the broken glasses on. Puts a tampon in her ear piercing.

ZODWA makes the area tidy – like a 'good' woman. She takes the rest of the rubbish, puts it back in the black plastic bag and throws it over to the rest of the rubbish.

She picks up the bin and starts to make different shapes with it – trying to find a correct image of womanhood through a dance movement sequence. All of the movement travels backwards or sideways.

The dance ends in a toi toi (protest dance) and then a fast spin in which she spots the dress hanging up.

ZODWA lands the bin down and sways, recovering.

CHARLIE enters from stage left and sways, as if reeling from shock.

ZODWA stands on the bin and starts to take down the dress as CHARLIE approaches the mic again.

SCENE – ORDINARY PEOPLE

CHARLIE goes to the mic. Looks at the audience/guests and does not know what to say. She closes her eyes and starts to sing 'Ordinary People' by John Legend, hesitantly at first, then building.

Meanwhile ZODWA is dressing on top of the bin. With her back to us she removes her T-shirt. Under her T-shirt, her breasts are bound with bandages. She removes the bandages. She puts on the jacket and the skirt. She removes her boxer shorts. She has flesh-coloured pants on beneath the shorts. When she has finished dressing she turns around and gently joins in the chorus of the song below.

CHARLIE: Girl I'm in love with you

This ain't the honeymoon

The lyrics continue. ZODWA gently joins in the chorus and CHARLIE sings whilst turning to face her, in a kind of fantasy moment for CHARLIE, wishing ZODWA into reality.

We're just ordinary people

We don't know which way to go[2]

Lyrics continue until the end of the song.

CHARLIE: [I guess I'm just] killing time. That's our song, the song we chose for our first dance. We should really be dancing by now. I had a speech prepared but… *(Taking the unused speech from her pocket.)* I've been to three hospitals and there's no… Look I know you've all known Zodwa for a lot longer than I have and you're probably all thinking she's had second thoughts about getting married and emigrating to England and she's scared of flying and sometimes she hides herself away and of course yes she had doubts like anyone would but she wouldn't just stand me up. She wouldn't abandon me at the altar. *(Getting*

---

2   Music and lyrics by John Legend and will.i.am accessible here: https://www.youtube.com/watch?v=PIh07c_P4hc

very upset.) She wouldn't do that she wouldn't do this she wouldn't do it but no one is *listening! (Off mic, to someone in the audience.)* It's my wedding, I can say what I fucking like! I paid for it. *(Shocked at herself.)* Play 'Ordinary People'! Please. I'm going to report a missing person.

CHARLIE exits stage left again as the DJ plays the instrumental version of John Legend's 'Ordinary People'.

SCENE – ZODWA'S ARABESQUE

With the music as above, ZODWA goes through the poses from the magazine again, this time up on the bin. The moves are mixed with the butch lesbian identity that she had before, still trying to figure out how to be 'straight'/corrected. It is a physical battle between masculinity and femininity. An archetype of femininity – the delicate ballerina – wins. She turns in a circle, all the while on top of the bin. This movement transforms into ballet and ends on an arabesque balance on the bin.

ZODWA goes off balance.

She grips the bin, still with her leg in the air.

Her skirt falls over her head so all we can see is her bare leg stretched upwards.

ZODWA tries to figure out how to straighten her leg but cannot.

ZODWA: *(In English/Xhosa to the audience.)* Is it straight? Does it look straight?

She keeps asking the audience until she engages them in dialogue, all the while performing an arabesque.

Eventually she stands, with her dress still over her head, facing downstage. She almost looks like a statue of the Virgin Mary. She tries to stay straight and still as a statue.

Lights rise on CHARLIE as she enters from upstage left, returning to the mic.

SCENE – CHARLIE AND THE POLICEMAN

CHARLIE carries her apple and uses it, like a cricket ball, throughout the scene. Catching it, rubbing it on her thigh, like a stress ball. She speaks to the audience downstage left, while ZODWA is upstage right, standing on the bin.

CHARLIE: I've just come from the police station and do you want to know what the officer said? *(ZODWA plays the policeman throughout the scene from up on the bin as CHARLIE mouths the words. They do not look at each other.)* 'She probably went to find an African man to marry her instead.' I said, *what?* 'She cannot marry a woman, it's unnatural, this thing, this thing,' and slurps his tea. I said, 'We are supposed to be flying to London in an AEROPLANE. But I guess that's unnatural too, isn't it? People, flying in the sky like birds.' *(An aside to the guests.)* Zodwa always says…

CHARLIE turns to face ZODWA, as before with 'Ordinary People', in a tiny flashback moment of ZODWA speaking to CHARLIE.

ZODWA: If God had meant us to fly, he would have melted wax on our backs and fixed on feathers.

They both laugh.

During CHARLIE's next speech, ZODWA gets down from the bin and spots a cigarette and matches on the ground.

She picks up the cigarette, strikes the match on the wall and lights it.

She carries out a movement sequence conveying a memory of a cigarette being in her face, ash tipped on her head, and the cigarette being stubbed out painfully.

CHARLIE: We're going to miss our plane… The policeman says, *(ZODWA as policeman again.)* 'It's not our culture, it's not African'. I said, 'Well we are getting married today in an *African* church. But now that I think about it church isn't very African either is it? There's nothing African about Christianity. *(The DJ, apparently offended by what CHARLIE is saying, tries to interrupt her speech by bringing in dance music. It is 'Township Funk'. This gives CHARLIE all the more fight.)* Well Jesus was Jewish, except all the paintings make him look Dutch! Irony is, my parents, my "white adopted parents" that is, helped bring Christianity to this country. Met in Africa as missionaries in the 1960s. Spent their honeymoon soaking up the sun on whites-only beaches in Cape Town. Had a splendid time, and Daddy even made money in the mineral mines. Made an absolute killing in phosphorus.' *(ZODWA as policeman.)* 'What?' 'Phosphorus, you know, the stuff on matches? *(DJ gives up the battle and brings the music down slightly.)* I presume that's how a humble Vicar and his clinically depressed wife could afford to give a private education to an abandoned brown baby in Stratford-upon-Avon. Except all I was interested in was playing cricket *(Mimes a six hit in cricket.)* And *that's* how I got the chance to come to Cape Town myself, where I met my girlfriend – my fiancé: Zodwa Ndlovu, see. *(Showing a photo on her phone.)* 'andILovyu'. It's how I remember the spelling. I'm taking her name. Charlotte – Charlie Ndlovu. My birth mother actually named me Donna. I fantasise that my dad was in the West Indies cricket team. Donna Ndlovu. Got a ring to it, don't you think?' He doesn't even pick up his pen but gulps back his tea, licks his lips and proceeds to stare at my non-existent cleavage. I lean forward to give him a closer view: 'Yes my white daddy came back from South Africa whispering all sorts of stories about what the savages got up to in their huts. *(DJ, offended again, jacks the music back up.).* Oh sorry have I offended your African sensibility? You don't think white people invented sex like they did aeroplanes, do you? Sorry to disappoint you but apparently Africa is the cradle of civilisation so all these same-sex shenanigans must have started somewhere. I think you'll find that being a lesbian is as South African as your Rooibosch tea! *(CHARLIE almost starts rapping into the mic now.)* People like my parents imported *homophobia* – not homosexuality. And the Europeans brought all kinds of other clever inventions with them – concentration camps, genocide –'

ZODWA: *(Interjecting on the mic.)* Apartheid.

CHARLIE: 'Are those things African too?'

ZODWA: *(As policeman.)* 'It's in the Bible! It is forbidden!'

CHARLIE: 'Well so is eating PRAWNS! *(Really riding the music rhythms now, ZODWA gets closer to her, smoking, playing and dancing funkily and sexily with the cigarette, the mic stand and CHARLIE.)* Working on a Saturday, sitting next to a woman who's on her period and a baby boy still having a foreskin dangling after he's eight days old – not to mention biblical justifications for the slave trade – but let's pick and choose the rules shall we?! Stuff the tricky bits in Leviticus about menstruation, shellfish, slavery, Sabbath rest and excess penis flesh – let's persecute the sodomites instead! Well, I don't know about you but I've never been that into sodomy myself. No, I know, I have tried lubrication' – the officer's jaw drops open. 'But I hear anal sex is an excellent *heterosexual* contraception. You should try it sometime – but always use a condom won't you?'

Calming down, CHARLIE and ZODWA back away from the mic together as the music fades out.

The lovers go stage left, underneath the light bulb, to the area that is later ZODWA's shack.

They lie down together.

CHARLIE lies on her side, talking directly to ZODWA, as if they are in bed. This is a physical flashback, but the words are still in the present, as part of the scene with the policeman.

ZODWA takes CHARLIE's apple and takes a bite from it, eating in 'bed' as she is listening.

CHARLIE: *(Gently.)* 'Unnatural. I'll tell you what's really unnatural. Forcing your cock into a woman's cunt. That is unnatural. That is *un*-African. So are you going to look for Zodwa Ndlovu or not?'

ZODWA hands the apple back to CHARLIE.

Both CHARLIE and ZODWA lie back and fall asleep together for a moment. CHARLIE sits bolt upright with a gasp.

ZODWA disappears back up to the bin.

CHARLIE returns downstage right to the mic and the audience. She is a little shaken by the anger she conveyed to the policeman.

CHARLIE: Now the policeman doesn't seem too happy about my tone of voice. True, I could have been a bit more diplomatic, but it's been a very difficult day. And as the beads of sweat are crystallising around his crucifix he looks deep into my eyes... Deep into my eyes... And I have never felt so white. *(CHARLIE, deep in this thought and memory, turns around and looks at ZODWA, lovingly. She goes upstage and talks to her, but does not touch her. The text remains in the present moment, even though she is addressing ZODWA who is not really there.)* Most of the 'coloured' people I've met here seem to be proud of their whiteness, it's the bit they tell you about first – *(South African Cape 'coloured' accent.)* 'Ja my great-grandfather came from Wales.' *(CHARLIE rolls the apple off stage, as if she is bowling on a village green.)* Or whatever... But when you ask about the rest of the story, it goes quiet. Whiteness has always made me feel... inadequate. I wish I could...scorch it. I wish I was...

like Zodwa. I say to the policeman, 'I only came to this country to teach black girls how to play cricket. Do you like cricket?'

ZODWA: *(As policeman.)* 'Soccer.'

CHARLIE: Strangely disappointed, I go on… 'It was just a bit of fun, winter sun, bit of adventure, do some good, volunteer, see Africa… I didn't mean any harm. I fell in love, you know? *(CHARLIE backs away from ZODWA, watching her at a diagonal, from some distance.)* I watched her, watching me, watching the girls practice, and… I was stumped. She is *so* beautiful. And when she spoke, she bowled me over…'

SCENE – FLASHBACK: ZODWA AND CHARLIE'S FIRST CONVERSATION

From up on the bin, ZODWA speaks to CHARLIE, recalling their first conversation/flirtation.

ZODWA: Are you content to play with those white sticks and red balls, or do you want to learn to play another game?

CHARLIE: *(Through a slight laugh.)* What kind of game do you have in mind?

ZODWA: I think in English you call it 'hide and seek'.

CHARLIE: What do you call it?

ZODWA: One covers their eyes and calls 'ndize, ndize…' and the other hides and calls 'oye!'

CHARLIE: What does it mean?

ZODWA: *(Singing.) Ndize ndize.* Can I come? *(Singing.) Oye.* Not yet.

CHARLIE: *(To the audience/wedding guests, miming cricket.)* She knocked me for six! Far across that boundary. And what

43

a catch – 'HOWZAT?!' *(ZODWA sings the text below, crossing over CHARLIE's speech.)*

ZODWA: Ndize ndize, ndize nolulubhayi! Ndize ndize, ndize nolulubhayi! *(ZODWA starts to pull up her skirt singing sexily, playfully.)* Ndaqabisonka esine jam. Ndaqonduba ndiyarhala. Ndaqabisonka esine jam. Ndaqonduba ndiyarhala. Ndize!

CHARLIE leaps up and starts to play hide and seek with ZODWA behind her skirt.

ZODWA looks for CHARLIE around and under her skirt, but does not see her.

CHARLIE dives under ZODWA's skirt and lifts her off the bin. They run around in an upright '69' position laughing and calling 'ndize, oye, can I come, not yet!' etc.

CHARLIE lands ZODWA back on the floor.

ZODWA rolls away and hides.

CHARLIE continues to try and look for her whilst returning to the mic.

CHARLIE kneels at the mic.

ZODWA grabs the bin, balances it on her head precariously. She tries to keep control of the bin on her head but can't, whilst CHARLIE is calling the text below.

CHARLIE: Can I come? Can I come? I'm coming I'm coming I'm COMING!

ZODWA finally slams the bin down centre stage and stands on it with her back to the audience.

SCENE – CHARLIE AND THE POLICEMAN, PART 2

'Sanctus' from Fauré's 'Requiem' comes in, sung by an English boys' choir.

CHARLIE is on her knees, Christian prayer position, speaking into the mic, gently, over the choir music. CHARLIE's tone immediately totally changes, much more subdued, speaking to the policeman, close to the mic, quietly, with a great deal of irony.

ZODWA, with her back to the audience, immediately goes into a sharp, angular, gestural movement sequence drawing on cricket umpire movements, with something of the priest/dictator about her.

CHARLIE: The policeman says… 'I think you still have time to catch your plane back to England.' Ah yes, our pretty little island. We actually wanted to get married in my father's parish. Mum might have even got up from bed to bake us a cake. The only problem is Daddy is one of those angry Anglicans who stands in his pulpit on a Sunday morning to preach that gay marriage will destroy the Church of England. Ironic, coming from an institution that was started by Henry the Eighth – a man who murdered two of his six wives and broke from the Pope because he wanted a divorce. Still, he did invent cricket and that's evidently all I'm good for. Poor Dad, and he thought he was singeing his white guilt by adopting a little half-breed nigger like me. What a disappointment I turned out to be. What a waste of all those minerals. So we would have got married in England, but we can't.

Fauré music snaps out, a switch in tone.

ZODWA starts to frantically look through the helium balloons. She is looking for evidence, looking for the culprit. She is starting to realise what has happened to herself.

CHARLIE is now more upbeat. She takes the mic stand off and moves in the space with the mic in her hand, like a stand-up comedian.

CHARLIE: Personally I blame the Royal family. You see if they legalise gay marriage it would mean a queen could marry a queen. Then where would we be? No no no, a faggot in the royal family would end up as dead as a… Dodi. That would be even worse than Princess Diana marrying a Muslim! They'd have to put the brakes on that one. *(She makes a screeching sound.)* So that's why we decided to get married here, in South Africa. *(Sarcastic.)* The rainbow nation, symbol of forgiveness and reconciliation, where equal rights are enshrined in your glorious constitution. Except it's not that simple, is it? So tell me, nice Mr Policeman – where are we supposed to go? Well perhaps I should thank you, if this were Nigeria, Uganda or just about anywhere else in Africa – *I'd* be the one under arrest. He jangles his keys. Are you going to look for her? *(Silence.)* WHERE IS MY WIFE?! Go home… I think everybody should just… Go home. *(CHARLIE exits.)*

By the end of this speech, ZODWA has found a flaccid balloon and a black felt tip pen. She stands on the bin, centre stage, blowing up the balloon.

SCENE – ZODWA CONFRONTS THE MURDERER

ZODWA blows up the balloon until it is the size of a human head. She proceeds to draw a face on the balloon, describing the features of the face:

ZODWA *(In Xhosa.)* Little eyes. Big nose. Dry lips. Afro. Moustache. Big ears.

ZODWA looks at the face. She holds it up again and has a good look. She turns the balloon slightly, making sure it is him; the audience can then also see the face at a point. ZODWA's rage builds through her speech, but it is still very internal with plenty of space between thoughts.

ZODWA: *(English.)* I stand corrected. Is this what you wanted?

(Xhosa.) You fucking bastard.

(Xhosa.) Are you happy now?

(English.) Are you happy with what you see?

(Xhosa.) This was supposed to be my wedding day.

(Xhosa.) Did you pay *lobola* for me?

(English.) Did you pay the bride price?

(English.) Was I worth it?

(Xhosa.) Did you choose the right one, between me and my sisters?

(Xhosa.) Did alcohol open the way?

(English.) I did not say 'I do'. I do? I do?

(Xhosa.) No, I definitely did not say 'I do'.

(English.) Words got stuck in my throat…

(Xhosa.) What about you?

(English.) Did you make vows?

(English.) Did you give cows?

(English.) Who was the best man?

(Xhosa.) The very best?

(English.) Who gave me away?

(Xhosa.) Did you pay for the damage?

(English.) You started it. Finish it.

(Xhosa.) You started it. Finish it. You started it. Finish it. You started it. Finish it.

(English.) You cannot divorce yourself from this. There will be consequences.

(Xhosa/English.) What God has put together / let no man set asunder.

(Xhosa.) There can be no divorce.

(English.) There can be no divorce.

ZODWA now takes the balloon in both her hands and presses it hard over a sustained period of time until it bursts with a bang.

White-out; sudden bright lighting state. Then blackout. ZODWA moves to the back wall in the darkness.

CHARLIE comes on in the blackout. We hear the sound of her wheeling a suitcase with balloons and cans trailing from it.

SCENE – BACK IN ZODWA'S SHACK

On blackout, CHARLIE strikes a match, stage left, as if she is looking for a light switch. She finds it and the bulb comes on.

CHARLIE enters. She has changed out of her wedding outfit and is wearing a casual honeymoon outfit. It has a hint of 'cricket' about it, with chinos, sports T-shirt, blazer and soft shoes. She walks slowly, wheeling on a yellow honeymoon suitcase with her. Attached to it are cans and balloons. There is a red L plate sign on the side (standing for learner driver or lesbian).

She turns on the light and pauses to look at the naked bulb.

ZODWA watches CHARLIE from the back wall.

CHARLIE cannot see ZODWA.

CHARLIE pauses to look around the shack. There is nothing left in the shack, as they were emigrating. She doesn't know what to do with herself.

CHARLIE removes her jacket.

She decides to open the case and look in the scrap book/engagement present ZODWA made for her, looking for clues to what happened. She calls as she flicks through the pages.

CHARLIE: Ndize ndize, ndize nolulubhayi…

Silence.

CHARLIE: Ndize ndize…

ZODWA: Oye.

Startled and confused, CHARLIE looks around to see where the sound has come from. She thinks she must be hearing things.

She continues flicking through the scrapbook, swaying.

ZODWA sways behind her.

ZODWA tries to put her hands over CHARLIE's eyes. CHARLIE doesn't notice.

ZODWA 'magics' the light bulb on and off and starts to move it.

CHARLIE drops the book, frightened.

ZODWA touches CHARLIE's aura, though not her body.

CHARLIE can sense a presence but does not know what it is. She starts to enjoy it but then is suddenly spooked and starts to respond shaking it off. She looks as if she is possessed for a moment.

Trying to calm her down, ZODWA reaches inside the suitcase and takes out a bottle of her own perfume.

ZODWA sprays perfume in the air. CHARLIE recognises ZODWA's scent. She smells the scent, closing her eyes.

ZODWA sprays the perfume all along the back wall from stage left to right.

CHARLIE follows the smell.

SCENE – LOVE-MAKING DREAM

Music – 'Ndize' by Zahara.

CHARLIE slowly begins rolling along the wall from left to right, smelling ZODWA's scent. ZODWA does the same from right to left. Their movement along the wall is reminiscent of making love. After some time they meet in the middle and hold each other.

CHARLIE and ZODWA hold each other for a long time, upstage centre. They turn a small circle like a slow dance. They kiss sensually centre stage.

ZODWA starts to pull away; she must go to her grave. They hold each other, pulling from the arms, to the hands, into a low counter-balance. CHARLIE resists ZODWA's leaving.

Eventually, when they are just clasping by the fingertips, CHARLIE lets ZODWA go.

ZODWA, walking backwards, lies down on the open suitcase.

CHARLIE crumples to the ground, sobbing her heart out.

SCENE – MEMORIAL SERVICE FOR ZODWA

CHARLIE opens her eyes as ZODWA is leaving, but does not see her go.

CHARLIE takes a black handkerchief from her pocket and ties it like a 'dook' (scarf) around her head.

She goes over to the mic on the ground, in the same position as it was for the wedding.

She picks it up, speaking slowly.

CHARLIE: And so the time has come, in this magical memorial, to say exactly what happened to our friend, my beautiful bride-to-be… At the trial they said… *(The voice of the Black South African radio announcer immediately takes over with the text below, but there is simultaneous action described here.)*

ZODWA walks slowly over to CHARLIE and takes the mic, then goes to sit on the bin downstage left. ZODWA begins to explain what happened to her on the mic, except we cannot hear her voice at all. Instead we hear the radio announcer. The voice-over is underscored by the sound of rain.

Whilst the voice-over continues and ZODWA mouths her story, CHARLIE looks back to the suitcase. She removes a piece of dark cloth that has been sitting on top of the contents of the case.

She wraps the cloth around her waist. It is a skirt.

CHARLIE is now the picture of a grieving widow.

CHARLIE starts to take the wedding presents and boxes out from inside the case. In a ritual-like action, she places them around the space, making a graveyard.

RADIO ANNOUNCER: …Zodwa Ndlovu was walking back from the local shop where she bought a box of matches. The man stopped her in the alley and asked her for a light. She knew him from the neighbourhood. She lit his cigarette. After whatever words that were exchanged, he grabbed her throat, pushed her up against the wall and choked her. She passed out and hit her head on the way down. As she lay, dying, the killer invaded her body. Then he stubbed out his cigarette on her genitals. He texted his friends to come and do the same and filmed it all on his mobile phone. That's what got him six years in jail. When they were finished they emptied out a rubbish bin and put her body in. Then they tried to destroy the evidence, starting by setting fire to her feet. But it started to rain…

The sound of rain builds.

ZODWA exits, stage left to right, still mouthing her story on the mic.

CHARLIE has finished laying out all the presents/graves by the end of the speech. She stands amongst the graves/presents, reading her memorial service speech from a piece of paper.

CHARLIE: I remember there was a great storm that night, as if the heavens were raging. I imagined the winds sweeping through the bars of Robben Island's prison cells, where once *great black men* in the fight for freedom dwelt: Walter Sisulu, Lionel Davis and Madiba himself. I couldn't sleep with fear and excitement. I wanted to jump in a taxi and go to her because I know heavy rain on corrugated iron is so loud and I was sure she wouldn't be able to sleep either. But we had agreed to spend the night before our wedding apart, as is the tradition. So I slept soundly under the white crisp sheets of my luxury Sea Point hotel bed and covered my ears with a soft pillow. The men ran through the rain, ran away as she smouldered… *(End of written speech. Rain dies out. CHARLIE looks at the 'graveyard'.)* Why?! Why are so many men doing this? Something must have sparked this flame, something must have fanned this flame, something must have started this fire. There must have been phosphorus. *(Pause.)* English-owned phosphorus… *(CHARLIE goes downstage left to the bin and turns it over, where ZODWA was sitting earlier. She takes her matches out and starts to burn her written speech, thinking out loud…)* In the English game of cricket, at the Oval cricket ground, the highest prize is the ashes, remains of bails, two little pieces of wood that rest between the stumps. The ashes are all I have. I told you I came here to teach cricket. I think I really came here to find my roots. And I found an ancestor, in Zodwa. She was the wisest, brightest, most poetic person I ever met. Born of a mother whose waters broke in protest *(gesturing to a woman in the audience as if ZODWA's mother is there)* and a father forced to stay far from home, coughing up his life in the mines. Parents who sacrificed everything so Zodwa could be the first girl to graduate as a lighting technician. They may have stubbed out her flesh but they can never extinguish her light. *(A beat.)* I am told that, amongst her people, you can have an ancestral wife. That's who I'll be. If she will have me. If you will join us. If you will be our witness. *(CHARLIE comes downstage and takes her position again at the 'altar', as before. She gently sings 'We Have All the Time in the World', the song from her wedding march, whilst collecting her flowers from the audience member who took them at her exit before.)*

CHARLIE: We have all the time in the world
    If that's all we have, you will find,
    We need nothing more…[3]

During the song ZODWA enters, in a slow march, from upstage right, along the white pathway, as CHARLIE did before, but walking backwards. ZODWA has the same costume as before but also wears a veil. CHARLIE's song ends. They stand together.

SCENE – THE WEDDING

The brides face each other. CHARLIE uncovers ZODWA's veil to reveal her face.

ZODWA: *Sibiza unkulunkulu*

CHARLIE: *Sibiza unkulunkulu*

ZODWA: *Nabantu bonke balapha*

CHARLIE: *Nabantu bonke balapha*

ZODWA/CHARLIE: We call on God and these people here present

CHARLIE: to witness that I – Donna

ZODWA: to witness that I – Zodwa

---

3 From 'We Have All the Time in the World' by Louis Armstrong. Accessible at https://www.youtube.com/watch?v=RMxRDTfzgpU

CHARLIE/ZODWA: do take you, to be my wife.

ZODWA: *Ukafa akuyonto*

CHARLIE: *Ukafa akuyonto*

ZODWA: *Uthando lulutho*

CHARLIE: *Uthando lulutho*

ZODWA/CHARLIE: Love is stronger than death. Love is stronger than death.

They kiss.

They turn.

They pause.

Together they throw the flowers behind them, as brides do at weddings.

An audience member/guest catches the flowers.

Blackout.

THE END

Curtain call: the protest song from the opening plays, this time more celebratory, without the sound of rain.

THE SINISTER ADVENTURES OF…

ASARA AND THE SEA-MONSTRESS

…IN THE KINGDOM OF DEXTER DEXPHORIA

Asara and the Sea-Monstress was researched and developed in 2011/12 through the Birmingham REP and Unicorn Children's Theatre Emerge programme with Caroline Jester as Dramaturg. The play had the first full staged reading at Albany Theatre on 1 August 2014 with the following creative team:

Creative Team

PRODUCER / WRITER / DIRECTOR MOJISOLA ADEBAYO

DESIGNER RAJHA SHAKIRY

COMPOSERS CONRAD KIRA, JUWON OGUNGBE

MUSICIAN JUWON OGUNGBE

STAGE MANAGER ALISON POTTINGER

MARKETING DEBO ADEBAYO

Performers

WITCH Y ANN AKIN

WITCH Z JACQUI BECKFORD

TOSHUN / MAMA ASARA ANTONIA KEMI COKER

SUITOR / BARRISTER BRUNO CORREIRA

LORD LAND / SPORTS TEACHER DAVID ELLINGTON

PAPA ASARA / FARMER CHARLIE FOLORUNSHO

WITCH X ALISON HALSTEAD

KING DEXTER / YAGI JOSEPH JONES

ASARA AMAKA OKAFOR

NB: All the performers (except Amaka Okafor) also played various other ensemble roles listed below.

With thanks to all the children and young people who gave invaluable feedback on the play between 2012 and 2014. Thank you to Georgia Folorunsho, who stepped in from the audience during the first performance to play the Majit, the cat.

Style

Asara and the Sea-Monstress is envisioned as a multisensory epic storytelling theatre production that re-imagines Yoruba, Danish and Greenlandic myths, folk-tales and fairy stories, with integrated British Sign Language. It is pitched at children, approximately four to ten years old, though it is very much a show for all ages. It is to be played by a multi-skilled, culturally diverse ensemble of actors who also sing, move, use sign language and puppeteer. A key element in storytelling is the integration of projected hand-drawn animation. This may be used to illustrate the setting but is also part of the dramatic action at specific points.

Setting

The play is set in the mythical Kingdom of Dexphoria, in a town on the edge of a forest, close to a river leading to the sea. The location is reminiscent (but not a replica of) Yoruba land in Nigeria during the late colonial era. It is somewhere like historic Oshogbo, a town beside the sacred river and forest of Oshun, the river goddess in Yoruba mythology.

Characters and casting

As the play is set in Nigeria, the cast should go some way to reflecting the African heritage and context of the work, though not to the exclusion of actors from other backgrounds. Where possible, the cast should be culturally diverse, including physical disability and sensory impairment. Actors can be doubled as appropriate. The named characters, in order of appearance, are as follows. Italics indicate where lines are sung or chanted musically.

WITCHES X, Y & Z

All three are in disguise at points, engaged in the whole action. WITCH Z is also the sign language interpreter who expressively interprets the show, interacting with and observing the action in every scene, in role. Though she has the main responsibility for communicating the play in this language, other players can also use sign language where appropriate. WITCH X or Y can be played by a D/deaf actor, as can any of the roles below.

PAPA ASARA
ASARA's father, called PAPA.

LORD LAND
The landlord of ASARA's family home and consort to KING DEXTER.

MAMA ASARA
ASARA's mother, called MAMA.

ASARA
The heroine; seen at birth, age three, six and eleven.

DEXTER
Crown Prince and later King of Dexphoria.

FARMER
He appears in a story told by PAPA to ASARA. The FARMER is father to TOSHUN and he is also LORD LAND's younger brother. FARMER is played by the same actor as PAPA.

TOSHUN
FARMER's daughter. TOSHUN is played by the same actor as MAMA. The 'o' in TOSHUN is pronounced as the Anglo-English way of saying 'orange'. TOSHUN transforms into the SEA-MONSTRESS.

SEA-MONSTRESS
A giant puppet operated by the actors who play COURTIER, SUITORS, CHILDREN, DESIGNERS and TOWNSPEOPLE. She is described in the play.

SUITORS
Three suitors to TOSHUN. These actors also play CHILDREN, TOWNSPEOPLE and DESIGNERS.

YAGMAI (known as YAGI)
ASARA's best friend, the same age as her.

CHILDREN
Three children in ASARA's school, aged eleven years old.

TEACHER (of English)
Can be played by the same actor as DEXTER.

SPORTS TEACHER
Can be played by the same actor as LORD LAND.

COURTIER
Servant to King DEXTER.

BARRISTER
For the prosecution. Can be played by the same actor as LORD LAND.

GUARD
Of the prison tower.

MAJIT
A fluffy black cat; a puppet.

Act One

Pre-show: there is instrumental West African music playing. As the lights go down, projected animation takes us to the Kingdom of Dexphoria. We travel from the sea, along a river beside the busy little town and out to a stream flowing through a magical forest. We settle on a clearing. Three WITCHES enter through the audience. They play percussion instruments. Their costume is open to interpretation but their left hands are certainly decorated distinctly. They arrive at the clearing in the forest and begin a ritual, calling on their goddess…

WITCHES: Sea-Goddess, said Monstress, our salt water mistress

We sinister sisters, insulted as wretches

Seasons on seasons, exiled in the forest

Oh swim from the sea, up river to this stream

Your face is our sunrise, your wish is our dream

Send us a sign in which we can trust

Send us a saviour! For justice – for us!

Oh send us a saviour, send us a sign, send us a sign…

WITCHES hear the footsteps of a man whistling, walking purposefully through the forest. It is PAPA ASARA. WITCHES scatter as he emerges, watching him from behind the trees. He notices the remnants of their ritual by the stream, and runs scared through the forest, arriving at the river. WITCHES follow him.

SCENE – PAPA FISHES

PAPA ASARA sits on the bank of the river, fishing with a rod. His net is empty. WITCHES watch him. LORD LAND, puffy and wealthy, approaches behind him with a shotgun directed at his head. WITCH Z interprets what is said, through BSL, for the other WITCHES and simultaneously for the audience.

LORD LAND: Red-handed!

PAPA drops the rod and net and prostrates before LORD LAND.

PAPA: Lord Land! I was just –

LORD LAND: – poaching in my river!

PAPA: I know it looks bad but –

LORD LAND: *(Pushing PAPA towards the river with his gun.)*
    You'd make great crocodile bait. I could make new shoes
    from you…

PAPA: I beg you I –

LORD LAND: Shut up, get up and put up your fishing licence.

PAPA gets up.

PAPA: But I can't afford one…

LORD LAND: Thought as much, thieving wretch. No one
    is allowed a catch without a permit stamped from King
    Dexter of Dexphoria! And *we* don't want rats like you –
    hang on, don't I know you?

PAPA: Yes Sir, my wife and I rent a little hut from you, but
    we've fallen on hard times and –

LORD LAND: Even the tribe-on-the-other-side is bust. That's
    no excuse for theft!

PAPA: I would have paid you back. I could have invited you
    round for stew!

LORD LAND: Sounds fishy.

PAPA: My wife is about to give birth but she hasn't eaten a
    fish in a whole moon. We've waited all our lives for this
    moment and now there's nothing left for the baby in her
    belly. Take pity.

LORD LAND: Take them off.

PAPA: Sir?

LORD LAND: Your sandals.

PAPA: But they're the only ones I've got.

LORD LAND: If you're so poor how come you can you afford shoes?

PAPA: You want me to walk barefoot?

LORD LAND: Those ten toes trod on my turf. Every time you look down at your dirty little worms wriggling in the mud you'll regret what you did. Now get them off before I throw you and your fat wife out of your hut!

PAPA: She's not fat, she's pregnant!

PAPA hurriedly undoes his sandals. The SEA-MONSTRESS rises from the river, behind PAPA. LORD LAND can see her but PAPA has no idea she is behind him.

LORD LAND: WOWOOAAH!

The SEA-MONSTRESS plucks the shotgun from LORD LAND's trembling hand and sticks it in her wild hair, like a hairpin. PAPA offers LORD LAND his sandals.

LORD LAND: MONSTRESS!!!!

The SEA-MONSTRESS rages at the insult. PAPA checks out his toes.

PAPA: You really think they look like worms?

LORD LAND flees sans sandals! PAPA picks up his fishing rod and looks despondently into his empty net. Suddenly the SEA-MONSTRESS spits a huge fish from her mouth, over the top of PAPA's head, which lands in his fishing net. She dives back down into the water again.

PAPA: A FISH! My life! *(Remembering.)* My wife!

PAPA runs home with the fish. WITCHES emerge, delighted.

WITCHES: *(Laughing then chanting.)* He he he he he! Sea-Goddess! Give praises! Hear Lord Land cry – 'monstress!' He couldn't be more scared if he was in Loch Ness!

WITCH X: Let's sneak to the city, put on disguises. *(Starting to change costume.)* Give Lord Land 'n' King Dexter some'more witchy surprises.

WITCH Y: Spying to see our saviour arrive! For this must be a sign!

WITCHES: This must be the sign! Ha ha haaaaaaah… *(Their laughter becomes the screams of MAMA ASARA giving birth. They follow the sound.)*

SCENE – ASARA'S BIRTH

PAPA and MAMA ASARA's hut, inside a walled compound. PAPA dashes on with the big fish in his arms. WITCHES X and Y are coming out of the hut, carrying a bowl and cloths, badly disguised as midwives.

PAPA: *(In BSL and speech to WITCH X.)* Did I miss it?

MAMA ASARA, sitting up in bed with the baby, calls from inside.

MAMA: Where have you been?!

PAPA: *(Calling back.)* Catching dinner! *(Showing the fish to the 'midwives'.)*

WITCH Y: Your firstborn has brought you luck it seems.

PAPA goes in, surprised and delighted. WITCHES X and Y hide outside, watching the action through a window. WITCH Z sits in the corner of the room with MAMA.

MAMA: *(Softening.)* Lucky those midwives were passing by.

They smile tenderly at each other.

PAPA: Can I hold…

MAMA: Her.

The smile at each other.

PAPA: Daddy's girl! *(PAPA takes ASARA and gives MAMA the big wet fish. ASARA takes PAPA's finger.)* She's a strong one! *(To the midwife.)*

WITCH Y: She came out hands first.

MAMA: Like she couldn't wait to touch the world.

PAPA: Then we must call her 'Abirtha' – 'about one whose birth there is a story'.

WITCH X: Asara.

PAPA: What's that?

MAMA: I suspect it means 'troublesome'.

WITCH Y: She certainly gave us some trouble.

MAMA: Asara. Sounds pretty though, don't you think?

PAPA: What about our tradition? We can't just pluck a name from the sky! *(ASARA starts to scream at his raised tone.)* What shall I do?

WITCH X: Tell her a story.

PAPA: Which story?

WITCH Y: Think.

A beat.

PAPA: Now, be a good girl, not like naughty little Toshun, the beautiful girl named after the river, who returned to it as an ugly monster!

MAMA: Can't you tell her a nicer story?

PAPA walks with the baby and continues the story.

PAPA: A long time ago there was a kind farmer with only one daughter, Toshun, which means 'the river gave me'. Her mother came from the tribe-on-the-other-bank but she died from malaria. So the farmer was soft on Toshun for she was all he had. He wanted her to marry a rich man so she could live in comfort and –

MAMA: – pay him a big fat dowry, exchange his daughter for a sack of money…

PAPA: He wanted her to be a *happy* wife. Many rich suitors came to woo, but Toshun said…

SCENE – TOSHUN

Projected animation instantly takes us from the hut to the farmer's well-to-do house in the story. PAPA immediately plays FARMER and MAMA plays TOSHUN. TOSHUN has short hair. WITCH Z continues to interpret but now she is up on her feet, in role as an interpreter in a storytelling performance.

TOSHUN: NO! I DON'T WANT TO GET MARRIED!

FARMER: We've been through all this before –

TOSHUN: – I'm only twelve I want to play!

FARMER: Toshun you shall do as I say.
    You will marry and you will be gay
    with a frilly white dress and a shiny wedding ring –

TOSHUN: – but that silly stuff doesn't mean a thing –

FARMER: – on this family there will be no disgrace.
    Stick a smile on that sulky face and meet the suitors I have arranged.

TOSHUN: I don't want to marry *any* man! Not now NOT *EVER!*

FARMER: Won't you just meet them Toshi, be nice for daddy.

TOSHUN: Nice? All you care about is the bride price! Can't you see I am busy playing with my toys!

FARMER: Those toys are for boys and you're too old for playing games.

TOSHUN: Well you bought them for me so who's to blame?!

FARMER: Toshun, for shame! You'll put me in the grave. You will learn to behave. You are spoilt. You want me dead like your mother? Then you'll feel guilt! *(TOSHUN cries. FARMER instantly regrets what he said.)*

FARMER: Toshi… *(Cuddling her.)* Just do as I say and the tears will dry up like the stream in summer.

TOSHUN: *(Still really upset.)* But I don't want to meet the stupid suitors…

FARMER: *(Tenderly.)* They aren't stupid.

TOSHUN: *(Instantly recovering.)* How do you know?

FARMER: *(Stumped by this.)* Well…

TOSHUN: You wouldn't want me to marry a fool, would you… Daddy dearest…?

FARMER: I only want you to have what's best.

TOSHUN: Well how about I set them a test?

FARMER: What kind of test?

TOSHUN: Nothing that my own clever father couldn't solve…

FARMER: Go on…

TOSHUN: The one who can fulfil my threefold task, won't even have to get down on one knee to ask, we will exchange our wedding bands and whoever he is – I promise you daddy –

I will give him my hand –

FARMER: – in marriage! At last! Send in the first suitor!

SUITOR enters.

SUITOR: – get on with it!

TOSHUN: Stay locked in my father's barn, from sundown 'til sunrise –

SUITOR: – easy! –

TOSHUN: – NAKED –

SUITOR: – oh –

TOSHUN: – and don't move a muscle when the mosquitos bite! I need man with his feet firmly on the ground.

SUITOR: Is that it?

TOSHUN: The morning after, you must eat my homemade hot pepper soup for breakfast, without blowing a single breath to cool your burning tongue. I need a man who can take the heat under pressure.

SUITOR: No problem!

TOSHUN: Lastly, you must sing one song to the whole community from midday to midnight. I need a husband who can win the ear of the town, who is creative, skilled and most of all has stamina.

SUITOR: Bring it on!

SCENE PLUS ANIMATION – SUITORS' TESTS

This scene is conveyed rapidly in projected animation. We see the SUITORS in the barn. They try to keep still and endure the bites, but almost all end up twitching and then slapping their bodies furiously, thus failing the first part of the test. Two manage to stay still and endure the mosquito bites. They come out of the barn in the morning. FARMER looks hopeful. They can hardly walk. One tries the hot pepper soup but it burns like hell and he can't eat it without blowing. The next succeeds but then breathes fire (literally) and runs off screaming. He runs through the forest and dives into the river. The townspeople laugh. TOSHUN is delighted. FARMER is distraught. End animation.

PAPA: None of the suitors could pass the test and so the Farmer was very worried.

MAMA: He was running out of money.

SCENE – LORD LAND AND DEXTER VISIT

We see FARMER in his house, which is more tattered than before. Downhearted, FARMER counts the last of his cowries. TOSHUN is playing happily with her toy vehicles. WITCH Z is still interpreting as before. Knock on the door. Nothing. Another knock.

FARMER: Where's that blasted house-boy?

TOSHUN: You haven't paid him.

FARMER: Well you better answer it then.

Another persistent knock. TOSHUN reluctantly gets up. Enter the (soon-to-be) LORD LAND, younger than we saw him before, much slimmer and dressed well.

LORD LAND: Toshun, not married yet?

TOSHUN: *(Reluctantly, formally greeting through kneeling.)* Uncle.

FARMER: Oh, run out of money already? I see you've bought yourself some new clothes.

LORD LAND: The robes were a gift from a new acquaintance with high taste.

TOSHUN: You look very pretty, Uncle.

LORD LAND glares at TOSHUN, then to FARMER.

FARMER: Go and bring your Uncle something to drink.

TOSHUN: *(Sarcastic sweetness.)* Would you like to try my hot pepper soup?

FARMER: Water!

TOSHUN exits.

LORD LAND: She must have got that attitude from her mother. They have no reverence for their elders on the other side.

FARMER: What is it that you want?

LORD LAND: I have recently become favoured by royalty.

FARMER: *You?*

LORD LAND: Crown Prince Dexter and I have become… associates. The King naturally wants to see the Crown Prince Dexter married before he dies. He has promised to bestow riches on the family who can provide a bride. Of course I told him all about my sweet little niece.

LORD LAND opens the door. Enter the flamboyant Crown Prince DEXTER.

FARMER: Your Royal Highness! *(FATHER prostrates in formal greeting.)*

DEXTER: Quit the ceremonials, let's cut to the matrimonials. I've got a fitting for my wedding outfit at two – I can't wait! Farmer, your young brother tells me that you have a daughter…

FARMER: TOSHUN! Yes Crown Prince, see –

Enter TOSHUN with drinks. DEXTER barely looks at her.

DEXTER: Girls all look the same to me, but I'll take your word for it. I understand all the suitors of the land have failed to win her hand.

FARMER: Yes sire, there is not a man in all of your father's kingdom who has been able…

DEXTER: We'll see about that.

LORD LAND: There's no need for you to perform this silly test –

TOSHUN: – that's not fair!

LORD LAND steps on TOSHUN's foot.

TOSHUN: Ow!

FARMER: Keep quiet.

DEXTER: I wouldn't want people to think I was too dim to do it. And people might say I was chicken, and you know how I can't bear birds! *(LORD LAND impersonates a chicken, DEXTER feigns camp fear, flaps his arms about, they laugh. TOSHUN and FARMER look on bemused – this must be some kind of private joke.)* Anyway, it'll be fun. The fitting can wait. But first we'll have to make a few changes around here. I can't possibly marry a girl from a scruffy farmer's family. So I declare you… *(Taking out his sword and anointing FARMER with it.)* Right Honourable Minister of Agriculture. And my dearest friend, how would you like to become Lord of all this Land?

LORD LAND & FARMER: *(Surprised and excited.)* Thank you Your Highness!

DEXTER: *(To TOSHUN.)* Now, kid, what's this stupid test…?

TOSHUN: See how you cope without swatting the mosquitos.

SCENE – DEXTER'S FIRST TEST

DEXTER is naked in the barn. Clever blocking conceals his privacy. LORD LAND whispers instructions into his ear. DEXTER starts talking in a very expressive way, slapping himself to punctuate his speech, thereby swatting mosquitos. This can be improvised by the actor to find as much humour as possible, something like this…

DEXTER: Well *(Slaps thigh.)* this is easy *(Claps hands together.)* I can't believe I *(Slaps his chest.)* of all people was so worried *(Slaps his cheek.)* about how I would do this *(Slaps forehead.)* And it's actually great fun! *(He claps himself wildly again, swatting lots more mosquitos. LORD LAND joins in with the clapping.)* It's a bit hot in here though, LL you wouldn't be a dear and pass me my fan? *(LORD LAND gives DEXTER his horse-tail fan. We see LORD LAND sneak some corn from the ground into his pocket. Animation shows time passing, the sun rises.)*

PAPA: And that's how Dexter survived the night. And in the morning…

SCENE – DEXTER'S SECOND TEST

DEXTER comes out of the barn in the morning. LORD LAND whispers instructions to DEXTER on how to manage the next task. TOSHUN presents DEXTER with hot pepper soup, convinced that he won't be able to manage this task. LORD LAND sprinkles corn that he has stolen from the barn onto the ground near DEXTER's feet. The chickens (puppets operated by the cast) gather around pecking the corn.

TOSHUN: Hot pepper soup for breakfast!

DEXTER: Uh cackly clucky flippy flappy things. I can't abide birds! Get away while I sup some soup. *(He sips the soup and between mouthfuls shoos the chickens, thereby blowing his mouth cool.)*

(Sips the soup.) Shooooo… *(Sips the soup.)* Shooooo… *(Sips the soup.)* Shooooo…

TOSHUN takes the empty soup bowl, distraught.

PAPA: And that's how Dexter survived the morning. And all day long…

TOSHUN: You must sing one song to the whole town!

SCENE – DEXTER'S THIRD TEST

The TOWNSPEOPLE gather around for the song. DEXTER is worried about this part; he doesn't know any songs and he is a terrible singer. LORD LAND gives DEXTER ideas through gestures, conducting him. He shows him the grains. DEXTER tries to keep the song / story going for as long as he can.

DEXTER: There was once a farmer that had a grain store
But no matter the harvest he always wanted more and more and more…
He could not understand why there was never enough grain
He asked himself over and over and over again…

LORD LAND mimes an idea for DEXTER – a mouse.

DEXTER: Little did he know that there was a clever little…mouse!
Who crept into the grain store at the back of the house
And each night on his back he balanced a grain and the mouse would do this over and over and over again…

73

LORD LAND: And the next night?

DEXTER: He took another grain.

LORD LAND: And the night after that?

DEXTER: He took another grain…

FARMER: The sun has set! He's done it! Prince Dexter will be King and my daughter a Queen!

TOSHUN: NO!

LORD LAND: That spiteful little kitten needs a beating! Doesn't she know how rich we will be!

TOSHUN: If you lay one hand on me I'll…

FARMER: Toshun, you must honour your word.

TOSHUN: You really want me to marry someone I cannot love?

DEXTER: Don't worry my dear, I love myself enough for both of us.

FARMER: The Prince has made me a Minister, he has made your uncle a Lord and you a Lady. We can't go back now. Imagine all the dolls you can play with when you are Queen.

TOSHUN: Father, you are right. I promised that I would give the winner my hand and that is exactly what I am going to do.

Instantly back to PAPA narrating the story.

PAPA: And with that, Toshun drew the sword from Prince Dexter's sheath and cut off her left hand!

TOSHUN holding up her bloody hand, visually enhanced through animation.

TOSHUN: AAAAAAAAAAAAAH!!! THERE! You have my hand! Stick the ring on the finger yourself!

MAMA interrupts herself telling the story.

MAMA: Enough now, husband, she's too young for such a
story! You're scaring her.

ASARA giggles happily.

PAPA: See, she's enjoying it!

*Back to the action. TOSHUN's arm is sprouting sinews and nerves
where her hand once was. It's gruesome.*

SCENE – TOSHUN'S TRANSFORMATION
(WITH ANIMATION.)

PAPA: Toshun ran through the forest. All the townspeople
chased after her. Toshun bent down to bathe her bloody
stump in the water but she fell into the river! Her father
died of a broken heart. Dexter declared: 'From this day
on, the left hand shall be a warning to all who betray me.
Banish the left-handed! Throw their belongings into the
sea!' And at the bottom of the sea Toshun transformed
into a Sea-Monstress. The sprouting sinews of her
left hand became an octopus. Her hair became green
seaweed. Her eyes – jellyfish. Her nostrils – sea shells.
Her mouth is a mussel. Her feet are two crawling crabs
and her remaining right hand is a flapping fish. And that's
how a pretty little girl became a Sea-Monstress.

MAMA: And the *moral* of this sordid tale?

PAPA: Errr… A girl must always do as her father says…!
Ah look she's grinning.

MAMA: I don't think she's grinning dear, I think she's
grimacing…

*Huge poo-ing sound. Visuals of the baby's grimacing face and the
baby's grumbling. ASARA does a huge poo that leaks all over PAPA.*

PAPA: URGHHHH!

MAMA *(Touched and proud.)*: Ahhhhh! Asara's first poo! Good girl!

ASARA giggles.

MAMA: Six years later…

SCENE – KING DEXTER'S PROCESSION

PAPA, ASARA and the WITCHES (badly disguised as ordinary happy citizens) are in the crowds, in the town square, waiting for the King's procession to pass by. Some of the scene can be set by animation. Music off stage comes closer and closer until he arrives. ASARA is older now, around six years old.

PAPA: He's coming!

ASARA: I can't see!

PAPA lifts ASARA up to sit on his shoulders.

ASARA: Papa, what's that?

ASARA points with her left hand to a hand, fixed on a spike, on top of a high tower, overlooking the square.

PAPA: That's the prison tower – for criminals.

ASARA: But what's that thing on top of the tower?

PAPA: You remember that story I tell you every year on your birthday?

ASARA: The one about the girl who didn't want to get married?

PAPA: Yes. Toshun. Well *that* is the hand she chopped off. Preserved in *palm* wine – ha!

ASARA: Urgh!

PAPA: King Dexter made sure her left hand stayed up there as a warning. *(PAPA takes ASARA down and talks pointedly to her.)* That's why you mustn't use your left hand. It's a sin, okay? Only for dirty jobs.

ASARA: Only dirty jobs.

PAPA: Yes.

ASARA: Like wiping my bum-bum.

PAPA: Asara!

ASARA: How do I get my right hand clean if I don't rub it with my left hand? And how do I get my left hand clean if I don't scrub it with my right?

PAPA: Here he comes!

WITCH X: Oooh wonder what he'll have on this time.

WITCH Y: Oh he'll be trussed up like a peacock as usual.

WITCH X: Are you implying our imperial leader is *vain*?

WITCH Y: *(Sarcastic.)* Would I…? No, I love royalty, me. It's the very *fabric* of our society. Though it would be nice to get a glimpse of the *real* him… Don't you think?

WITCHES all look at each other, winking with their left eyes. They clock an idea for later. The crowds cheer and call compliments about how good he looks. The King's procession enters with musicians. LORD LAND leads the way, with his shotgun over his shoulder. The crowd cheers and all the people clap, but only with their right hands, thus making no sound.

ALL: Long live the King! Blessings on him! Long may he reign!

ASARA: King Dexter! Look down here! Here I am!

ASARA waves vigorously and excitedly at the King, with her left hand, and also clapping both hands together. Suddenly the music stops in discord as the King's procession clumsily halts. DEXTER glares at ASARA's hand.

DEXTER: What is the meaning of this?!

PAPA sees ASARA's left hand outstretched in the air.

PAPA: Lord Land, your Majesty, I am so so sorry.

ASARA: What's the point of only clapping with one hand?

PAPA: *(Whispering in ASARA's ear.)* Scream loudly when I pretend to hit you. Okay?

ASARA: Why?

PAPA: Just do it! You naughty little girl – take that!

PAPA makes a false display of punishing ASARA. It should be very comical bad stage combat! ASARA screams very loudly and reacts very physically, totally over the top, as if she is being murdered. PAPA and ASARA are not coordinated and get the screams and hits in the wrong places. She thinks this is all very funny.

PAPA: I have punished the offending hand, Your Majesty.

DEXTER: Make sure for your sake that it doesn't happen again.

LORD LAND steps aside to talk to PAPA.

LORD LAND: You owe me some fish stew, don't you?

PAPA: Oh yes, the fish! *(PAPA goes to take off his sandals. LORD LAND is irritated and embarrassed in front of everyone.)*

LORD LAND: – NOT NOW IDIOT! I shall call round on Friday evening and we can discuss your rent rise.

LORD LAND rejoins the procession. PAPA is very frustrated at the bad news.

ASARA: That was funny Papa, can we do it again?

PAPA, annoyed, grabs ASARA's hand and holds it tightly. ASARA squeals.

ASARA: Ow! Papa you're really hurting me! Papa I'm not pretending this time! *(With that, PAPA pulls the cloth tight. WITCH Y grabs PAPA's hand.)*

WITCH Y: If you hold her hand, tightly like that, it will only make a fist…

PAPA drags ASARA away. She looks back at WITCH Y, who winks with her left eye and waves a witchy wave with her left hand.

ASARA'S SONG

WITCHES: Head up
Don't be ashamed to be different
Head up
You can be whoever you want to be
Asara, you're special
As special as me
Hands up
If it's okay to be different

ASARA: Hands up if it's okay to be me

WITCHES: Asara, you're special
As special as me
You won't find a fingerprint that matches Asara's
You won't look in the mirror and see anyone but you
Don't hide
Be who you are
Inside
And you'll go far
It's different strokes
For different folks
And you were born that way…

79

You were born that way…
Hands up, head up, head up…

SCENE – HIGH SCHOOL

ASARA is eleven years old, in her new school. We are in a traditional West African classroom as it was during the colonial era. Various CHILDREN including YAGMAI (YAGI) at their wooden desks, in rows. A blackboard up front where TEACHER stands. WITCH Z is interpreting as MRS COUSINS, the classroom assistant. YAGI is listening to music on headphones, mouthing the lyrics of his song – lyrics below.

TEACHER: Welcome to your new class. You! *(Gesturing to YAGI.)*

YAGI: Sorry Sir, did you say something?

TEACHER: NAME!

YAGI: *(Taking his headphones off.)* Yagmai. Y-a-g-m-a-i.

TEACHER: Well at least you can spell. Never let me see you wearing headphones in English again! Have you got that straight?

YAGI: Yes Sir.

TEACHER: Now, calligraphy. Let's start with 'A' as in…

ASARA: Asara?!

TEACHER: Come along.

ASARA goes to the front of the class, upstage. TEACHER hands her a piece of chalk. ASARA writes 'A' on the board, very beautifully, but with her left hand. TEACHER and the class gasp loudly.

ASARA: I know, lovely isn't it? I taught myself! I try to imagine a snow-capped mountain, like they have on the other bank. I've never seen snow – have you, Sir? Shall I show you my 'S' too? *(Goes to write.)*

TEACHER: NO! I have not seen snow and I have no desire to see any student of mine write *like that*. Write 'A' again with the NORMAL hand.

ASARA: But it is nor–

TEACHER: The OTHER hand, Asara.

ASARA writes 'A' with her right hand, really badly. CHILDREN laugh.

TEACHER: Sit at the back with that hand under your bottom!

CHILDREN giggle. YAGI watches. ASARA goes to the back of the class, downstage. Another child gets up to write 'B'. ASARA sits on her left hand and attempts to write with the other.

ASARA: But Sir! It feels WEIRD!

CHILD 1: *You're* WEIRD!

CHILDREN laugh.

TEACHER: Stop showing off and use the proper hand like everyone else.

ASARA: I'm not showing off, I am just being me.

TEACHER: Well don't!

ASARA: But Sir it feels really odd, like I'm bent all back to front!

TEACHER: Well then, turn around and face the back when you write, maybe that way you'll feel better!

ASARA turns around, back to the class, facing downstage.

CHILD 2: *(Whispering.)* Keep up Asara, you don't want to get *left behind,* ha ha ha!

ASARA: *(Protesting about CHILD 2.)* SIR!

TEACHER: As you are being such a big baby you can draw pictures while the others write and I'll give you extra homework tonight instead: fifty lines –

ASARA: – that's not fair!

TEACHER: I agree – make it ONE HUNDRED LINES! *(TEACHER writes on the board:)* RIGHTLY IT IS RIGHTEOUS TO WRITE WITH MY RIGHT. IF I WRITE WITH MY RIGHT I WILL BE ALL RIGHT!

ALL: RIGHTLY IT IS RIGHTEOUS TO WRITE WITH MY RIGHT. IF I WRITE WITH MY RIGHT I WILL BE ALL RIGHT! RIGHTLY IT IS RIGHTEOUS TO WRITE WITH MY RIGHT. IF I WRITE WITH MY RIGHT I WILL BE ALL RIGHT!

TEACHER: ROUNDERS!

SCENE – THE PLAYGROUND

TEACHER: Yagmai! Yagi! *(Lifting his headphones.)* You're batting.

YAGI: But Sir I'm practicing my –

TEACHER: Stop being a sissy!

ASARA: *(Signing to him.)* Good luck.

YAGI: Thanks.

YAGI does badly – he's out on strike three.

TEACHER: Useless! Give the bat to Asara. You can keep score instead.

YAGI: Result!

TEACHER: Asara, now's your moment. Give it your all. Keep your eye on the ball and hit it as hard as you can. Got it?

ASARA: As hard as I can.

YAGI: GOOD LUCK!

ASARA smiles gratefully at YAGI then goes to bat. The CHILDREN improvise jeers – 'I'm not touching the bat after her,' 'Err,' etc. – and snippets of words from the song. Big music build-up. Animation visuals support. CHILD 1 pitches the ball. ASARA swings with her left hand.

TEACHER: THE OTHER WAAAAAAAAAAAAAAY!

It's too late. All the fielders run in the opposite direction than they expected and out of their positions. The ball smashes a school window, visualized through animation and sound effect. The English TEACHER from the previous scene screams from the window.

TEACHER: ONE THOUSAND LINES!

CHILDREN: *(Singing.)* Back-handed
　　Gibble-fisted
　　Scoochy-skiffy
　　Dolly-pad
　　She's growing up-sideways
　　And we all think she's mad!
　　Backwards and cack words
　　Any which way she's backwards
　　Lop-handed
　　Geeky fingered
　　Skivvy-cat-claw
　　Keggie-pug
　　She's all inside out guys
　　Just look at her mug!
　　South North West East words
　　Any which way she's backwards
　　Cack-handed

Gammy-fisted

Skew-wiffy

South paw

She draws with the hand that washing Ars-ara's for!

Clicky clappy

(Clicks/claps.)

Is she happy?

Clicky clappy

(Clicks/claps.)

In your nappy!

SCENE – THE DINNER GUEST

MAMA is frantically preparing for the arrival of the dinner guest. WITCHES are peering inside the hut from up on the roof. Enter ASARA.

MAMA: Where have you been? We've got a guest coming for dinner!

ASARA: I was playing with my new friend. He's soooooo lush, he's got curly eyelashes and turny-up lips...

MAMA: *(Glaring disapprovingly.)* Stir the stew, you.

ASARA: But I've got a thousand lines to write.

MAMA: What have you done this time?

MAMA takes the spoon out of ASARA's left hand and puts it in her right hand. MAMA holds her right hand over the top of ASARA's right hand for a moment, as she stirs, leading her.

MAMA: You'll find life much easier if you swim in the same direction as all the other fish.

MAMA releases her hand and goes to lay the table. ASARA stirs and thinks.

ASARA: Mama...

MAMA: Yes, love?

ASARA: Do you think maybe I'm like, a freshwater fish in salty water?

MAMA: Mm?

ASARA: Or maybe I'm a fish *out* of water.

MAMA takes the spoon from ASARA and puts it down.

MAMA: I think you've stirred that dish enough.

ASARA goes to get her book to start practicing writing by the fire. Enter PAPA and LORD LAND.

PAPA: You see Sir, it is a very humble dwelling. Not much space considering how much we…

LORD LAND: Let's eat first and discuss the rent later. I'm famished.

PAPA: Of course.

MAMA and PAPA look nervously at each other. MAMA brings the pot over.

MAMA: Asara. Table.

ASARA comes over to the table, bringing her book with her.

MAMA: For what we are about to receive we thank the creator –

LORD LAND: – and Dexter his King. Amen.

PAPA indicates that his wife should serve the food. MAMA serves the stew tentatively. ASARA starts writing the punishment lines again, muttering them to herself.

MAMA: It's fresh fish –

PAPA: – from the market.

LORD LAND: *(Sarcastic reference to the poaching incident.)* Where else?

PAPA is embarrassed. The adults start to eat uncomfortably around the tiny table. ASARA keeps writing awkwardly with her right hand. The writing slopes; frustrated, she blurts out.

ASARA: Rrrrrrr I can't write straight!

MAMA: Asara come to the table.

ASARA: But I've got another nine hundred and ninety-six –

A look from MAMA.

ASARA: Sorry.

ASARA puts the pen down, picks up the spoon with her left hand and bumps the stew into LORD LAND's lap, scalding him.

LORD LAND: Aaaaaah!

PAPA: ASARA!

MAMA: What have you done?!

MAMA mops LORD LAND's lap.

ASARA: I'm really sorry. Look, there's still some left – *(ASARA goes to serve him with her left hand.)*

LORD LAND: – LEFT!

MAMA: Can't you do anything RIGHT?!

PAPA: Go and do your homework over there!

ASARA: But –

MAMA: Do as your father says!

ASARA goes off to the side to continue writing her lines with her left hand. Frustrated, she starts to draw with her left instead, hiding the fact. She draws a beautiful flattering portrait of LORD LAND. We see the animation projected whilst the grown-ups talk. MAMA clears things away.

LORD LAND: I shall have to go home and change.

PAPA: I am sure I can find you something to wear.

LORD LAND: Certainly not! I had enough trouble last time with you and your shoes.

PAPA: Why *did* you run off like that?

LORD LAND: – forget it! I stink of fish, let's get down to business. The Kingdom's coffers are empty, we are in debt to the tribe-on-the-other-side and to top it all the King's Jubilee is next month. Taxes are going up and so is your rent.

MAMA re-enters on the last line.

MAMA: But we can't afford to pay any more!

LORD LAND: We must all do our bit to help celebrate.

PAPA: My wife is right.

LORD LAND: Well if your family weren't so sloppy, spilling soup everywhere, you might have more cash to spare. From next month it's double or you're out. *(LORD LAND goes to leave.)*

ASARA: Sir…

PAPA: Not now.

ASARA: But I drew a picture of you…

LORD LAND takes the picture roughly. He is impressed.

ASARA: …to say sorry for the stew.

LORD LAND: I look almost regal. *(LORD LAND goes to leave. MAMA and PAPA look at each other in despair about the rent rise.)*

LORD LAND: *(To PAPA.)* Have you considered entering the girl in the competition?

MAMA: What competition?

LORD LAND: To paint the King's portrait in his new Jubilee gown. The best likeness will be unveiled before the whole town. There is a handsome prize…

PAPA: How much?

LORD LAND: Enough to cover your rent for a while…

LORD LAND exits.

PAPA: Well Asara, what do you say?

ASARA: Great! All I need is paint. I've only got white.

PAPA: Black and white. There. *(Handing it to her.)* The last of my shoe polish!

ASARA: Well, let's hope the King's wearing zebra skin!

PAPA: I can't magic the money, Asara. We have to prioritise.

MAMA: We'll buy you more paints when you win the prize.

ASARA: But how am I going to win with wall paint and shoe polish!

MAMA pours what she's been mixing into ASARA's palette.

MAMA: Here! Will this do for now?

ASARA: *(Unimpressed.)* Yellow – wow.

MAMA: Egg yolk and turmeric. What do you think?

ASARA: First white, then black and now yellow – *(Sarcastic.)* Great! Maybe he'll be dressed like a big bumblebee?

ASARA runs around buzzing like an angry bee.

PAPA: You're behaving like a spoilt brat!

ASARA: I'm not a brat I'm a bee! See! Bzzzzzzz bzzzzzzzz…

PAPA: Then I'll have to swat you.

PAPA snaps and goes to hit ASARA. MAMA grabs his hand just in time. PAPA and MAMA start to row loudly over the top of her head. ASARA comes out from between them, carrying her paint palette.

MAMA: Stop it! She just wants to do her best.

PAPA: What, and you're saying I don't?

MAMA: Well you haven't exactly been lucky.

PAPA: What, did I raise the taxes? Did I put up the rent?!

MAMA: You didn't exactly protest! All that bowing and scraping…

ASARA: Stop fighting!

SCENE – DEXTER'S NEW CLOTHES

The palace. Animation may lead us there. DEXTER is viewing various clothes in the throne room, presented by various DESIGNERS. WITCH Z is disguised as a ROYAL INTERPRETER. LORD LAND's picture, painted by ASARA, hangs on the wall.

DEXTER: *(To DESIGNER 1, bearing beautiful robes.)* No, no, NO. Talk about *gauche.* You don't honestly expect me to wear *that* for my Jubilee?

COURTIER shows in DESIGNER 2, presenting another set of beautiful robes.

DEXTER: Oh p'lease – *passé!* My subjects expect me to lead them with a sense of *style. (To LORD LAND.)* It takes their sorry little minds off the recession.

COURTIER shows in DESIGNER 3 with another set of robes.

DEXTER: I said I want to look *hip,* not like a hippopotamus! I am supposed to be having my portrait painted!

COURTIER shows in DESIGNER 4 with another set of robes.
DEXTER shouts before he can even see them.

DEXTER: THAT'S IT! SORT IT, COURTIER, OR YOU'LL
BE FOR THE CHOP!

(DESIGNERS exit, bewildered. COURTIER exits, stressed.
DEXTER turns to LORD LAND for comfort.) Oh LL, I despair,
I won't have anything to wear… I must look magnificent,
mesmerising, I want to convey a sense of… MAGIC!

On the word 'magic', COURTIER opens the door to present WITCHES
Y and X, dressed as bohemian designers.

DEXTER: Who they?

WITCH Y: We've just flown in.

WITCH X: Graduated from the Stick-Broom design school.

WITCH Y: It's very high-flying. We are based across the river
in Ditch-Shore.

DEXTER: Hmmm, they look quite boho I suppose.

LORD LAND: *(Suspicious.)* Hmmm…

WITCHES: Hmmm…

LORD LAND: Well, what have you got?

WITCH X: We will create the most magical robes the King has
never seen.

DEXTER: That's exactly what I've been looking for!

WITCH Y: We work by moonlight –

WITCH X: – and the clothes will only be revealed moments
before they are to be adorned.

WITCH Y: It's part of the mystique.

WITCH X: Very chic.

LORD LAND: Sounds a bit risky to me.

DEXTER: Shush, I do like games. So, what will be so special about this outfit? I need something really cutting edge.

WITCH Y: We will make for you robes that can only be seen by the eyes of the very brave and the very wise… Only those who are intelligent and courageous – like you…

WITCH X: Cowardly fools won't have a clue.

DEXTER: Oooh, how exciting! Tell the Courtier what you need and I shall see you in the morning for the portrait sitting! Come on LL! Let's celebrate with some palm wine.

LORD LAND exits watching the WITCHES.

SCENE – YAGI AND ASARA MAKE A PLAN

ASARA joins YAGI, who sits on the wall of the compound, mouthing to a song. He sees ASARA coming and removes his earphones. WITCHES continue as before.

ASARA: They're fighting again.

YAGI: I know, I had to turn up the music to block it out.

ASARA: We'll end up homeless and it's all my fault!

YAGI: What happened?

ASARA: I entered the palace portrait competition to win a prize to pay the rent, but we haven't got any money to buy paints.

YAGI: I wish I could help…

ASARA: There's going to be proper grown-up artists there and everything. Have you got any paints?

YAGI shakes his head no.

ASARA: What am I gonna do?!

ASARA is really upset. YAGI doesn't know what to do. He goes to put an arm around her and changes his mind. MAJIT the cat, operated by WITCHES, comes and runs itself along ASARA, purring, trying to comfort her.

ASARA: Hello fluffy.

YAGI: That's Majit! My grandma's cat. What are you doing so far from the forest? Wait – why don't we ask her!

ASARA: I hardly think a cat is going to have paint.

YAGI: No silly, my grandma.

ASARA: Is she a painter?

YAGI: No but I overheard my parents saying that she knows how to…get things…

ASARA: Is she a thief?!

YAGI: No! She's a – I'm not even supposed to know.

ASARA: Whisper it.

YAGI whispers.

ASARA: SHE'S A WITCH!

YAGI: Keep your voice down.

ASARA: Let's go to the forest and ask for her help.

YAGI: But we're not allowed in the forest.

ASARA: I'll just say I went to visit Yagi's family – and it won't even be a lie! Come on, I want to see what she's like!

ASARA runs off. YAGI hesitates, then follows.

SCENE – LORD LAND'S INSPECTION

WITCHES cut and sew. It's like a sweatshop, except there is no fabric. LORD LAND inspects. COURTIER enters carrying more bundles of fine materials. WITCH Z repeats instructions to COURTIER and text to LORD LAND, in BSL.

WITCH X: Put the golden thread over there, next to the silver lining.

WITCH Y: Where are the diamonds? We need them for the buckles at once! *(COURTIER dashes, pausing to catch his breath by the material they are sewing.)*

WITCH Z: What do you think?

COURTIER is not sure what to say, then speaks and signs.

COURTIER: It's very…unusual… *(COURTIER exits to bring back the diamonds.)*

WITCH Z: *(To LORD LAND.)* You're not saying much.

WITCH Y: What's the matter, don't you like it?

WITCH X: Perhaps it's not to Lord Land's taste…

WITCH Y: Or maybe you're having trouble seeing –

LORD LAND: *(Quickly.)* – well, I must say, it's quite the most exquisite thing I've ever set eyes on. Yes, the pattern, the flow and line…

WITCH X: And the colours?…

LORD LAND: Oh yes, er, the colours are… Yes it's all very… er…new.

WITCH Y: Well, let's hope the King likes it as much as you do!

WITCH X: If you'll excuse us, we have a lot of work to do before sunrise.

LORD LAND: Of course, I'll leave you to it then.

LORD LAND exits, looks back, quite worried and confused. The WITCHES continue working with small knowing looks to each other. LORD LAND secretly checks through the window to see if they are still working.

LORD LAND: *(To himself, also signing the essence of the text.)* I can't see a damn thing! *(He checks again.)* Nothing. Everyone's going to say I'm a stupid scaredy cat. I'll probably lose my title! I'll just have to keep up the pretence and hope that Dexter sees sense!

LORD LAND exits, bemused.

SCENE – THE MAGIC FOREST

YAGI and ASARA in the forest, created through animation. They are dressed in green camouflage. Moonlight. Spooky sounds. YAGI is humming his song.

ASARA: What's that you keep humming?

YAGI: I'm just drowning out the sounds. I could have sworn I heard snakes.

ASARA: Hold my hand if you like.

YAGI: You're all right. *(Humming louder as they go deeper into the forest.)* It's late…

There's no one here. Maybe she isn't a witch after all. We should go back.

ASARA: Just a little bit further. The moonlight is lovely on the stream, don't you think…?

ASARA flutters her eyelashes.

ASARA: Hum it again Yagi… The melody is lovely. *(Fluttering again.)*

YAGI: Have you got something in your eye?

ASARA sighs.

ASARA: Yagi, I think I –

YAGI: Shh! I can hear footsteps!

ASARA: Hide!

Enter WITCHES laughing, revelling in their bounty, tucked into their bosoms.

WITCH X: With these twinkly trickster's trinkets we'll decorate the shrine –

WITCH Y: – and make sacred offerings to the water's divine Sea Goddess – our Queen! She will be so pleased.

WITCH X: Especially when she hears about what everybody sees!

WITCH Y: Shush! Spies! *(They quickly hide the materials.)*

WITCH X: Come out of your hidey-hole, coward.

ASARA: Yagi go on, talk to her.

YAGI: Grandma…?

WITCH Y: Who sent you?

YAGI: Great Aunt Fi! I thought you were dead!

WITCH Y: Who says I'm not?

WITCH X: Stop it, you're terrifying him.

ASARA: Aren't you Mrs Cousins –

YAGI: – the teaching assistant!

WITCH X: Yagmai, what are you doing here?

ASARA: We could ask you the same question!

WITCH Y: What do you want?

WITCH X: Yagi, you shouldn't have come here, and you certainly shouldn't have brought a stranger. It's not safe.

WITCH Z: Now go!

YAGI: Come on, Asara. This isn't going to work.

WITCH X: Not a word to your mother!

YAGI waves bye-bye and so does ASARA.

WITCH Y: Hey! Do that again.

ASARA: What?

WITCH Z: *(Waving.)* Wave bye-bye.

ASARA waves.

WITCH Y: Did you see that?

WITCH Z grabs ASARA's left hand. Reads her palm, nods at WITCH X.

WITCH Z: It's her!

WITCHES: Asara…

ASARA: How do you know my name?

WITCH X: We've been waiting for you.

WITCH Y: We've been watching.

WITCH X: I was there at your birth.

WITCH Y: I was there when you were growing up.

WITCH X: This is your destiny.

YAGI: Grandma, Asara is my best friend in the whole world.

ASARA: Reeeaaally? *(Slushy again.)*

WITCH X: You pick your friends well, Yagi.

YAGI: She is supposed to paint the King's portrait for a competition, can you help?

WITCH X: The King will look a pretty picture in his new robes!

WITCH Y: And it's paints you need?

ASARA: Yes, I've only got these rubbish colours, I need more.

WITCHES discuss.

WITCH Y: All we can do is ask the Sea Goddess on your behalf. But first –

A kind of swearing-in ceremony. The WITCHES pile left hands on top of each other, ASARA's hand last.

WITCH X & Y: Do you promise to be honest, to always use your left hand, your left-sided heart and the whole of your art to only ever reveal the truth, and no matter what challenges you face, always *always* be true to YOU?

YAGI nudges ASARA.

ASARA: I do.

WITCH: Well, here goes. *(Cueing them for a sung incantation, ritualized movement.)*

INCANTATION SONG

WITCHES: Sea-Goddess, Sea-Goddess, she whom they call monstress
You who gives succour to all souls in dis-tress
You've sent us a saviour in which we can trust
Her name is?

ASARA: Asara!

WITCHES: And she's one of us
Left-handed and sometimes –

ASARA: – ambidextrous!

WITCHES: Now her family need a helping hand
Give us three colours to fulfil the plan!

Pause.

WITCH X: It's not working.

WITCH Y: She can't hear us. The bottom of the sea is a long
way away, you know. We need to be louder.

WITCH X: Bigger!

YAGI: Wait, what about… Them…?

ASARA: Could you sing and sign a magic spell to call the
Sea-Monstress for help?

AUDIENCE: YES.

*Words of the spell/song are projected. WITCHES teach the audience
the spell in song and sign.*

INCANTATION SONG (CONTINUED)

ALL: Without different colours life would be boring

AUDIENCE: Life is more than just a black and white story

ASARA: Our family needs a helping hand

AUDIENCE: So give us your colours to fulfil the plan!

*Repeat the song, underscored with music. The SEA-MONSTRESS
rides a giant wave that rushes from the sea (animation), to the
river, arriving at the stream where they are gathered. Cheering on
her arrival, the WITCHES fall to their knees.*

SEA-MONSTRESS: Here is my blood

(WITCHES remove a pair of scissors stuck in her arm; it bleeds, they cup the blood.)

With it make red.

Squeeze my sea-weed

(WITCHES wring her hair and collect the green dye from it.)

Now you have green.

Squid – squirt ink blue!

(Her octopus arm squirts blue ink; the WITCHES collect it as with the other dyes. Last line is directed at ASARA.)

And forever be true!

(SEA-MONSTRESS rides away on a wave.)

YAGI: WOW!

ASARA: Come back! That's only red, green and blue! I need more!

WITCH Y: Why, you ungrateful little –

YAGI: – you've still got the black, white and yellow.

ASARA: So?

WITCH X: Well, what do you get if you mix red and yellow?

ASARA: I don't know.

YAGI: *(Looking to the audience for advice.)* Does anyone know? Orange…?

WITCH Y: And if you mix red and blue?

YAGI: Purple?

WITCH X: Red and white?

YAGI & ASARA: Pink!

WITCH Y: See!

ASARA: All the colours of the rainbow! Thank you Sea-Monstress! Now come on everyone – to the palace!

All exit. Interval. Music.

Act Two

SCENE – PORTRAIT COMPETITION

DEXTER is changing behind rainbow-coloured curtains.

COURTIER: Do you require any assistance, Your Majesty?

WITCH X: *(Sing-song.)* Dexy Rexy, don't be shy…

WITCH Y: It's time to come out of the closet!

> *DEXTER emerges naked. His private parts are hidden, throughout the following scenes, through clever and playful blocking. He appears to be able to see the outfit. He looks very pleased with it indeed.*

WITCH Z: *(Wide-eyed.)* Your MAJESTY!

DEXTER: Well, what do you think?

WITCH X: Certainly our best work yet!

DEXTER: LL?

LORD LAND: Well, what do *you* think?

DEXTER: I asked first.

WITCH Y: Do you like what you see…? *(ALL look closely at LORD LAND.)*

WITCH X: Is it easy on the eye…?

WITCH Z: Give us your view…

LORD LAND: I can't see… I can't see… Any – any – any –

COURTIER: – way it could be improved, Sir?

> *LORD LAND is trying to speak but can't get any words out.*

DEXTER: What's the matter with you? You look like you've got a hot pepper soup on your fingers – say it!

LORD LAND: It's…like…a mirage: illusive, beguiling and transpar– transparen– translu– trans– trans–

COURTIER: – a transformation Sir?

LORD LAND: Yes, it's quite.

DEXTER: Are you all right?

LORD LAND: No. I think I'm blind– blind–

COURTIER: – blinded by its beauty!

LORD LAND: Yes I'm stunned! I mean it's stunning! Like looking straight at the sun first thing in the morning – glorious!

WITCH X: And how does it feel, is the movement good?

DEXTER: Well, it's quite…snug.

WITCH Z: Mmmm…

WITCH X: Do you mean to say it's too tight? Around your waist perhaps?

WITCH Y: Would you like us to take it out a touch?

DEXTER: No, that's fine, we wouldn't want the bottoms falling down, would we?!

ALL: NO! No, no… That would never do. *(Uncomfortable laughing etc., clapping one-handed.)*

DEXTER: Well, I'm ready for my portrait!

DEXTER poses against the backdrop of the curtains. COURTIER opens the door. ARTISTS enter bowing. They eventually look up. Various reactions: shock, bemusement, repressed hysteria, confusion, yet all of them pretend they can see DEXTER's clothes – except ASARA, who enters last.

COURTIER: I present King Dexter in his birthday suit. I mean – his Jubilee robes! An outfit that can only seen by the brave and the wise! The winning artist shall receive a prize in celebration of his illustrious reign!

DEXTER: How do you want me?

ARTISTS are confused, not knowing what to say.

ASARA: Standing up is fine, Your Highness.

DEXTER: Very good, I shall do my best to keep still, though it is rather chilly!

The ARTISTS draw furiously. Multiple impressions/interpretations are projected as animation. All of the ARTISTS draw what they pretend they can see, except ASARA, who draws the King as she sees him. DEXTER is not very good at keeping still. He keeps shifting. COURTIER does a good job of blocking him. LORD LAND walks around inspecting the artworks and stops at ASARA's painting, shocked. He pulls her aside discreetly.

LORD LAND: Don't I know you?

ASARA: Asara. The fish stew…

LORD LAND: Well, I am not sure your painting will do.

ASARA: *(Mortified.)* What's wrong with it?

LORD LAND: There's probably everything right with it. Here, take this. *(He hands her a bag of gold coins and takes the picture.)*

ASARA: But I haven't signed it!

LORD LAND: No one is going to see it anyway. Now scram. Buy yourself a bag of sweets and a gob-stopper too. Right?

ASARA: Left! *(She runs off.)*

SCENE – POPPING CANDY

YAGI and ASARA are sitting on the wall of the compound eating sweets. YAGI has a bag of Space Dust. WITCHES watch/interpret, close by.

YAGI: He wasn't wearing *anything?*

ASARA: Not a stitch! But everyone was pretending. You don't think the witches had anything to do with it, do you?

YAGI: I wouldn't be surprised. Well, now you've got plenty of money for the rent and all the Popping Candy we can eat. Happy?

ASARA: I suppose.

YAGI: What is it?

ASARA: I wanted to win the competition properly. None of it seems very fair. The Sea-Goddess is still stuck at the bottom of the sea. The witches are still banished in the forest...

ASARA stuffs some more sweets into her mouth. Pause.

YAGI: I really miss my Grandma. How can you miss someone you hardly know? But I do... *(YAGI eats some of his Space Dust.)*

ASARA: Still, at least we've got each other.

ASARA twinkles her eyes again.

YAGI: You know what...

ASARA: What?

YAGI: I feel all tingly inside.

ASARA: Do you?

YAGI: Like a million tiny meteors are exploding inside me! Like music in my belly!

ASARA: *(Gushing.)* Oh Yagi, I feel exactly the same.

YAGI: There's nothing like it.

ASARA: It's out of this world!

YAGI: Exactly – Popping Candy! Thanks Asara. See you at school!

ASARA is deflated. YAGI runs off happy.

SCENE – THE COMPETITION

COURTIER is presenting the paintings to DEXTER.

LORD LAND: Well how about this one?

DEXTER: No.

LORD LAND: This one?

DEXTER: No!

LORD LAND: This?

DEXTER: You must be about as fearless as a chicken with a brain the size of a grain if you think that any of this is a true reflection of my marvellous jubilee outfit!

LORD LAND: Rex Dex…

DEXTER: Don't Dex Rex me! You're turning into an irritating little mosquito. None of these paintings deserves the prize. I am going to have to hold SOMEBODY responsible. Is this really the best there is?

LORD LAND: *(Worried now.)* Well, there was just one more…

DEXTER: Why didn't you show me before?!

LORD LAND: It was painted by a mere child, a girl at that.

COURTIER brings on and unveils ASARA's painting. DEXTER is transfixed by it. He comes closer. Pause. LORD LAND is tense.

DEXTER: It's like a photograph! Look at the line, the colours, the flow of the robes. I'll make a marvellous display!

LORD LAND: *(To COURTIER.)* Get the kid to the jubilee, let's get this blasted prize out of the way.

SCENE – THE NEWS

ASARA's home, she combing MAMA's new dyed blonde hair into a funky big new style. PAPA is filling the holes in his shoes with bill envelopes. WITCH Z, dressed as a postwoman, watches through the window, interpreting. ASARA goes to sit and draw MAMA.

MAMA: Can I move now…?

ASARA: No! I want to draw you with your new hair-do. Mama sit still!

ASARA draws. WITCH Z knocks. PAPA receives the post.

WITCH X: Post!

PAPA: Not another bill…

WITCH Z continues watching/interpreting. WITCHES X and Y in the distance.

PAPA: Oh. It's addressed to you Asara…

ASARA opens the letter. MAMA looks at her hair in the mirror – shocked.

ASARA: I WON THE COMPETITION! *(ASARA is jumping up and down cheering. MAMA and PAPA are trying to hug her.)*

PAPA: Well done Asara!

MAMA: I'm so proud of you!

ASARA: I've got to tell Yagi!

MAMA and PAPA embrace. ASARA runs outside.

MAMA: I can't believe she's done it!

PAPA: We'll be able to pay the rent.

MAMA: And keep the house!

PAPA: I'll go and tell Lord Land right away.

MAMA: Come here first.

MAMA and PAPA kiss.

SCENE – HOLDING HANDS

ASARA runs outside to the compound wall, where YAGI sits listening to music. She shows him the letter.

ASARA: YAGI! We did it!

YAGI: You're amazing!

ASARA: I couldn't have done it without you and the witches.

YAGI: *(Reading the letter.)* Wow, you'll never want for anything again.

ASARA: There's only one thing I want right now.

ASARA puts her left hand on YAGI's hand, on his lap. He snatches his hand away.

YAGI: What do you think you're doing?!

ASARA: I just wanted to hold your hand.

YAGI: Why?!

ASARA: I thought, maybe you and me could be…

YAGI: Well I don't want to hold your hand, Asara. That's not what I want. Why do you have to spoil everything. Why can't things stay as they are?

ASARA: I was going to invite you to be my special guest at the Jubilee. But forget it. I'll go on my own!

YAGI: FINE!

ASARA: I thought you were different, Yagi.

YAGI: I AM different.

ASARA: No you're not. You're just the same. You don't want me to touch you with my left hand.

YAGI: It's not that!

ASARA: Yes it is, LIAR. I'll never be accepted the way I am. I might as well run away and live with the witches in the forest. I HATE you!

YAGI: Asara, wait!

SCENE – THE JUBILEE

DEXTER parades through the town, lapping up the attention. LORD LAND parades with him, looking very uncomfortable. The crowds cheer, clap one-handed and pretend to see the outfit. MAMA and PAPA cheer along but look at each other as if to say, 'Can you see anything? No! Me neither!' WITCHES are disguised TOWNSPEOPLE again, pretending to see/interpreting.

WITCH Y: What a revelation!

WITCH X: Those designers have done a fantastic job. Don't you think?

WITCH Y: Definitely. It's such a good look on him. He looks so…

WITCH X: *Natural.*

WITCHES suppress their laughter. DEXTER arrives on the podium, says a private word on the side to LORD LAND as he continues waving to the crowds.

DEXTER: Well, how do I look?

LORD LAND: Like a… *(Not knowing what to say.)* Peacock!

Big cheers from the crowd. DEXTER quiets them down.

DEXTER: Thank you, thank you, my loyal subjects, this is really too much. It gives me great pleasure to unveil the winning portrait and present the prize of one million Dextons.

Portrait is unveiled. MAMA and PAPA are quite shocked.

ALL: Ooooooooh…

DEXTER: To Asara Tenant, whom I hereby declare the first Artist Laureate to the Kingdom of Dexphoria.

ASARA steps up onto the podium with MAMA and PAPA proudly behind her. Applause. DEXTER notices the painting is unsigned.

DEXTER: But you haven't signed the painting, dear. This is your work, isn't it?
I must say when they told me a little girl –

ASARA: – of course it's my work!

PAPA: *(Discreetly cautioning her to be polite.)* Asara…

ASARA: I mean yes, Your Majesty. I would never ever cheat.

LORD LAND: The Royal Quill, Your Highness.

ASARA: It's okay, I've got my own special pen.

Cameras flash. ASARA signs the painting with her left hand. Gasps.

DEXTER: LEFT?!

ASARA: YES, I'm left-handed – SO WHAT?!

MAMA: Oh no…

DEXTER: It is a CRIME to be left-handed in my Kingdom! You disgusting little –

ASARA: ME?! At least I don't walk around the whole town WITH NO CLOTHES ON! YOU'RE NOT WEARING ANYTHING!

LORD LAND: Silence her!

ASARA: He's NUDE! RUUUUDE! *(To the audience.)* It's true, isn't it, everyone?

AUDIENCE: Yes!

ASARA dashes to get the full-length mirror as DEXTER interacts with the audience, improvising something like the following.

DEXTER: You're all stupid wimps! That's why you can't see anything! What would you know?! Yellow-bellied imbeciles!

ASARA: You are STARKERS and by the way – your reflection in the mirror is left-handed too!

DEXTER faints.

LORD LAND: Arrest her at once! Lock her up in the tower!

ASARA is arrested and bundled away. MAMA and PAPA try to fight for her but are pushed away. WITCHES look to each other, worried – this has all gone too far.

MAMA: Take your hands off my child!

PAPA: ASARA!

SCENE – THE PRISON TOWER

ASARA is in a prison cell in the tower. MAMA and PAPA are visiting. WITCH Z, disguised as a GUARD, watches over her, interpreting.

GUARD: One minute left – lefty! Ha ha ha...

PAPA: But can't you just pretend? For our sakes, if nothing else?

ASARA: I made a promise that I would always be true to myself.

MAMA: *(Moving towards her.)* Asara, do you realize what they'll do to you?

GUARD: No touching!

ASARA: I'll show them, you'll see.

PAPA breaks down.

MAMA: You're breaking your father's heart. What about being true to your family?

Come on, Yagi's waiting outside. Maybe he can talk some sense into her.

ASARA: I don't want to see Yagi. I –

YAGI is let in. ASARA turns away. MAMA and PAPA leave with a pleading look to YAGI. ASARA and YAGI sit silently for a moment. She doesn't look at him.

YAGI: What's the food like?

ASARA says nothing. YAGI stares out of the window, making small talk.

YAGI: It's quite a view up here... You might even see snow on the mountain... *(YAGI checks the GUARD isn't listening.)* Don't worry, I'm going to go and ask the witches for help.

ASARA: I can look after myself.

Pause. YAGI secretly takes out a bag of sweets.

YAGI: Do you want a sweet? They're your favourite.

ASARA: I eat with my left hand, Yagi. You don't want to get infected.

YAGI: I don't care what you do with your left hand –

ASARA: – yeah, right. I saw the way you reacted when I touched you. You're just the same as everyone else.

YAGI: It's not because you're left-handed –

ASARA: Yes it is! You nearly jumped out of your skin.

YAGI: – you're still my friend!

ASARA: Well, I don't want to be friends with a sissy who can't even bat a ball! *(YAGI is hurt. The real GUARD enters.)*

GUARD: Time's up!

YAGI: You don't understand, I'm –

GUARD: Oi, lefty! It's time to face the music.

SCENE – THE TRIAL

ASARA is on the stand. DEXTER is the Judge. COURTIER is a clerk. LORD LAND, MAMA, PAPA, YAGI, WITCHES X and Y and TOWNSPEOPLE watch from the gallery. WITCH Z is a courtroom interpreter. Audience are addressed as a jury.

COURTIER: How do you plead?

ASARA: Not guilty!

COURTIER: Barrister for the prosecution.

BARRISTER: *(Bows to DEXTER, turns to ASARA.)* 'Asara'. An unusual name. Apparently the origins are – *(Looking at his evidence.)* 'Troublesome, shifty, sinister – left-handed.'

ASARA: Well I didn't name myself!

BARRISTER looks up at MAMA and PAPA. PAPA glares at MAMA.

BARRISTER: Indeed.

ASARA: Anyway, it just goes to show, doesn't it?

BARRISTER: What?

ASARA: I've been this way since I was born.

BARRISTER: So you admit to being left-handed?

ASARA: I'm not a criminal! I demand my rights!

BARRISTER: Left-handedness is not a human right but a human *vice.* It is not normal.

ASARA: It's not normal to be right-handed – it's just COMMON. You're just jealous because I'm special but I bet there are loads of left-handed people out there – just like me!

AUDIENCE: *(A few brave people respond perhaps? Would be lovely if some people 'came out' as left-handed. If they do, BARRISTER will have to improvise some banter with the left-handed people in the audience like, 'Well, we will put you on trial next...' COURTIER/CLERK can eventually call the trial to order.)*

BARRISTER: You are an abnormal abomination with no sense of shame!

ASARA: *(To the 'jury'.)* Your heart beats on the left-hand side. Does that make you ashamed?

BARRISTER: We are not the ones on trial. Using your left hand is perverted!

ASARA: But WHY?

BARRISTER is uncomfortable, looks around. No one wants to say why.

BARRISTER: It's used for…dirty jobs.

ASARA: What jobs?

BARRISTER: Big jobs.

ASARA: Well let's ban them too, shall we?
(*ASARA marches and chants.*)
Ban bums, ban bums, prosecute all who poo!
If you do do-do, then we'll do for you!

COURTIER: ORDER!

BARRISTER: Left-handedness came to this land because of Toshun, that evil Sea-Monstress who disrupts the weather and deprives our people of enough fish to eat! Her mother came from the-other-side where this immoral behaviour should remain! Over there they even drive on the left side and read and write from left to right – it's absurd!

ASARA: Well maybe I should go and live with them then?!

MAMA: No, don't send her away!

ASARA: Why not, Mama? Life would be a lot easier. Do they clap with both hands there too because I quite like doing that as well! YAY! (*She starts clapping herself.*)

BARRISTER: You see, everything about this creature is unnatural!

ASARA: If it's so unnatural why do some cats eat with their left paws? Scratch with their left claws?

BARRISTER: Where is your evidence?

ASARA: Bring in Majit and I'll show you.

COURTIER: Call Majit the cat!

MAJIT the cat is brought in by WITCHES X and Y. MAJIT is given milk to drink. Anticipation as MAJIT drinks milk, then dips his left paw in the milk and licks it.

ASARA: You see! LEFT PAW!

YAGI: Way to go Majit!

COURTIER: Silence!

BARRISTER: Well this just proves that lefties are a lower form of species. This despicable practice is not acceptable in the human race!

ASARA: Well then I'd rather be a cat. *(She meows and hisses.)*

BARRISTER: A sign of witchcraft! She works against God!

ASARA: God made me this way!

BARRISTER: You are left-handed because you love to sin!

ASARA: You really think I'd go through all this for fun?!

BARRISTER: You are a show-off, an *exhibitionist.*

ASARA: At least I don't prance around in public showing everyone my privates!

DEXTER: I've heard enough! CHOP IT OFF! CHOP HER HAND OFF!!

MAMA & PAPA: NO!!!

ASARA is taken from the courtroom by the GUARD. She struggles and shouts, 'Let me go,' etc. ASARA is taken past a huge baying crowd – enabled by animation. ASARA is dragged up to the executioner's block. Crowds cheer. MAMA and PAPA wail and cry out for mercy. YAGI runs up to the WITCHES.

YAGI: YOU'VE GOT TO DO SOMETHING!

WITCHES: Sea-Goddess! See Goddess! Witness injustice! Witness injustice!

WITCHES start to pray. The GUARD blindfolds ASARA, secures her hand on the block, raises his axe. Gasps from the crowd as he swings… And then… A huge wave sweeps in, shown through projected animation.

WITCH Y: TSUNAMI!!!!! RUN!

WITCH X: SEA-GODDESS BE PRAISED!

TOWNSPEOPLE scatter.

YAGI: ASARA YOU'RE SAVED!

ASARA looks up from the block in shock.

LORD LAND: What about the girl?!

DEXTER: Lock her up!

LORD LAND: Come on!

The tsunami engulfs the town as ASARA is rushed to the tower. The Sea-Monstress emerges, raging, the puppet in wild movement. Animation of tsunami, rising waves, flooded houses and streets. MAMA and PAPA and are in a tree, people are up on roofs, struggling on rafts, etc.

SCENE – DEXTER'S FLIGHT

The palace balcony. WITCHES badly disguised as engineers try to get DEXTER to put on wings and fly from the palace to safety.

LORD LAND: Dexter we must hurry!

WITCH X: The very latest design, Your Highness.

WITCH Y: Original peacock feathers!

DEXTER: But I can't abide birds!

LORD LAND: We've got to get out of here.

DEXTER: Can't we sail?

LORD LAND: Of course not – the Sea-Monstress is in the water! Toshun will have her revenge on you once and for all!

WITCH X: They say she's not your greatest fan.

DEXTER: I suppose the feathers are quite pretty.

LORD LAND: Dexy darling PLEASE – hang on, there's only one pair.

WITCH Y: We only had time to do two wings.

LORD LAND: But I can't swim!

DEXTER: See you on the other side!

Animation of DEXTER flying off dressed as a big peacock. LORD LAND is swept away by the waves and eaten by a crocodile. DEXTER crashes into the mountain on-the-other-side.

SCENE – HELP FROM THE TOWER

YAGI is hanging from a rope as he climbs up the tower. He is almost at ASARA's window, reaching a hand up. ASARA looks down at him.

YAGI: Give me your hand!

ASARA: *(Bitter but slightly playful.)* You've changed your tune.

YAGI: HELP ME!

ASARA: I thought you didn't want to touch it.

YAGI: ASARA PLEASE!

ASARA pulls YAGI in through the tower window. He is soaked.

ASARA: What do you want?

YAGI: You've got to ask the Sea-Monstress to calm down. It's gone too far!

ASARA: I'm not even speaking to you. What you did hurt me more than anything they said about me in the courtroom. I trusted you!

YAGI: It's not that I didn't want to hold your hand.

ASARA: Yeah right…

YAGI: It's just that I know you really want me to be your boyfriend.

ASARA: Talk about VAIN! Think a lot of yourself don't you?

YAGI: I'm not stupid. Look, I think you're great, I really do. But the thought of having a girlfriend feels really…back to front. Like when you have to draw with your right hand.

ASARA: Oh, what, you mean you're gay?

YAGI: Probably.

ASARA: Why didn't you say?!

YAGI: You didn't give me a chance!

ASARA: I'm so sorry, Yagi. It was really wrong of me to treat you that way. Friends? *(YAGI offers his hand to shake; it's his right hand. ASARA offers her left playfully, then YAGI offers his left hand. They shake hands, laugh and hug. YAGI sees the waters rising outside the window as he looks over ASARA's shoulder.)*

YAGI: Asara look, the waters are getting higher! Our families are stuck in the trees! You've got to make her to stop, we've got to save them!

ASARA: But what can I do? Lord Land and King Dexter will have me chopped up!

YAGI: Haven't you heard? Dexter put on peacock feathers thinking he could fly. He crashed into the mountain on-the-other-side.

ASARA: No way?!

YAGI: And Lord Land got gobbled up by a crocodile. All he'll be good for now is leather shoes!

ASARA: Ew. And what about the witches?

YAGI: They're out on a boat trying to make the Sea-Monstress see sense, but she's obsessed with revenge!

ASARA: Okay, I'll give it a go. *(Calling out of the window.)*
Sea-Goddess, you saved me from King Dexter's injustice
I beg you, show mercy to all those in dis-tress
Take pity on the city, return our river to the sea
And I promise I'll fight for the oppressed to be free!

SEA-MONSTRESS comes to the window, really raging. Her voice is amplified and distorted underwater sound. The voice is TOSHUN's.

SEA-MONSTRESS: NO!
I've had enough of your requests!
I listened to the witches
I did my best
But it's not just Dexter –
I've had it up to here with the people of Dexphoria!
For all I care this whole town can go under!

ASARA: But what about all the goodness in this place?

SEA-MONSTRESS: There is *nothing* good about the human race!

ASARA: What about my mum and dad, the witches, what about Yagi, his family, what about me?

SEA-MONSTRESS: I'll give you a ship and you can all live at sea.

ASARA: But we're only human, we are bound to make mistakes.
What will happen then?
Will you turn the tides again?
What would it take, when will it end?
You've got to stop this eternal revenge.

A beat.

You've got to learn to forgive
Or you'll never be free.
You've got to listen when people say they're sorry.
Just like I'll do for the grown-ups, just like Yagi did for me…

SEA-MONSTRESS: But what they did to you was so wrong!

ASARA: I know… And I know it was the same for Toshun.

SEA-MONSTRESS cries at the mention of the name she had as a girl, for the first time since her transformation.

SEA-MONSTRESS: Tears…
I haven't been able to cry, not once in all these years…
I was so happy, playing with my toys, why did it have to change?…

She really grieves now.

ASARA: How about I paint you a beautiful portrait while Yagi sings you the song he's been working on –

YAGI: – WHAT??

ASARA: – will that make you feel better?

SEA-MONSTRESS: But look at my reflection! *(She looks into the sea.)* I'm so ugly!

ASARA: You don't happen to have any left-handed scissors, do you?

SEA-MONSTRESS: Yes! Hundreds! They've been sticking into me. *(She plucks scissors from her torso.)*

YAGI: *(To ASARA, desperate.)* Why have I got to sing? I can't –

ASARA: Come on Yagi. You've been mouthing the lyrics for weeks.

YAGI: How did you know?

ASARA: I've been looking at your lips quite a lot.

YAGI: *(Cringing, covering his ears with his headphones.)* Errrrrr!

ASARA: You've got to stop hiding away. *(Removes his headphones.)* It's about time you let people hear your voice. Now's your chance.

SEA-MONSTRESS: *(Handing the scissors.)* I'm a frightful mess but – do your best.

ASARA gives YAGI an encouraging look. YAGI sings whilst ASARA cuts the SEA-MONSTRESS' hair. The tune is gentle, simple. All the fish and sea creatures are freed from her locks. She has a funky new short haircut. ASARA draws her portrait as the song comes to an end.

YAGI'S SONG

YOGI: My name is Yagmai
Spelt Y-A-G-M-A-I
It could mean 'I am gay'
As mirrors seem to say
Or maybe I'm just
Shy
Whatever your name, whatever your thing
If they push you out or try to force you in
If they say you must play
Make up another game

Maybe you'd rather sing with me...
What would be the real shame is if we were all the same
Be who you want to be, you'll find a family
Your own happy
Sometimes to lose your way is your way of finding you
To be wrong, to fail, could be your way of being true
My name is Yagmai
Spelt Y-A-G-M-A-I
It could mean 'I am gay'
As mirrors seem to say
Or maybe I'm just
Shy
My name is, your name is, my name is...

The waters subside. All is calm. ASARA gives SEA-MONSTRESS the portrait.

SEA-MONSTRESS: Is that really me?

ASARA: I only ever paint what's true.

SEA-MONSTRESS: Thank you Asara, thank you Yagi! I'll treasure this forever!

In animation – a wave comes and the SEA-MONSTRESS rides away happily with the dolphins. A rainbow appears.

SCENE – BACK DOWN TO EARTH

MAMA, PAPA, YAGI'S MUM and DAD, TEACHER, WITCHES and TOWNSPEOPLE are gathered on dry land now. They call up to the prison tower. ASARA and YAGI are at the window.

ALL: Three, two, one, JUMP!

ASARA and YAGI jump down from the tower and they are caught by everyone.

MAMA AND PAPA: Asara!

MAMA: You're safe at last – I'm so sorry my darling.

PAPA: We'll never let anyone treat you that way again.

TEACHER: *(To YAGI.)* Thank you for rescuing us, Yagi.

YAGI: It's not me you should thank. Asara saved the day.

TEACHER: Thank you, and… I think I owe you an apology.

TEACHER offers her left hand to shake.

ASARA: You're left-handed too!

TEACHER: Yes, but I was so scared that I'd get the sack so
I kept it secret.

WITCH X and Y look at each other, remove their disguises.

TEACHER: *(Continues.)* Then when you came along and you
were so brave it made me even more terrified. I thought
if I made life hard for you I wouldn't be discovered. Can
you forgive me?

ASARA: Write me a thousand lines and I'll think about it.
(A beat.) Only kidding!

YAGI notices the WITCHES.

YAGI: Grandma!

PAPA: Auntie Fi! We thought you were dead!

WITCH Y: How do you know I'm not?

WITCH X: Stop it, you're scaring him.

WITCH Z unveils as MRS COUSINS.

MAMA: Mrs Cousins!

ASARA: All my favourite people! *(MAJIT meows – it sounds like 'and meee'.)* And not forgetting – Majit the cat! This is the best welcome home party ever. Tell you what I'd really like though. Could you all stand together, I want to treasure this moment forever.

They all stand together and sing whilst ASARA draws them. The animation is projected; the audience join in the song as before.

ASARA'S SONG

ASARA: Head up
Don't be ashamed to be different
Head up
You can be whoever you want to be
Asara, you're special
As special as me
Hands up
If it's okay to be different
Hands up if it's okay to be me
Asara, you're special
As special as me
You won't find a fingerprint that matches yours or Asara's
You won't look in the mirror and see anyone but you
Don't hide
Be who you are
Inside
And you'll go far
Cos you were born that way…
You were born that way…
Hands up, head up, head up…

THE END

ORANGES AND STONES

A PLAY-WITHOUT-WORDS
ABOUT LIVING UNDER OCCUPATION

Oranges and Stones began life as a ten-minute play-without-words for two performers called *10 Minutes for Palestine*, conceived, directed and designed by Mojisola Adebayo and co-devised and performed by Sukhesh Arora and Royana Mitra at Royal Holloway, University of London in the Spring of 2001. It was later developed into a full production with Ashtar Theatre (Palestine) entitled *48 Minutes for Palestine*, receiving its first full premiere at Ashtar Theatre, Ramallah, Palestine, on 4 May 2010, with the following creative team.

Creative Team

DEVISOR / DIRECTOR / DESIGNER / WRITER
MOJISOLA ADEBAYO

DEVISOR / PERFORMER PLAYING ISSAC / LIGHTING DESIGNER EDWARD MUALLEM

DEVISOR / PERFORMER PLAYING SAMAR RIHAM ISSAC

COMPOSER / MUSICIAN RAMI WASHARA

DEVISOR / UNDERSTUDY PERFORMER / ASSISTANT DIRECTOR MOHAMMAD EID

DEVISOR / UNDERSTUDY PERFORMER RASHA JAHSHAN

STAGE MANAGER MOHAMMAD ALI

Iman Auon became part of the team in 2017 as a devisor and performer playing SAMAR.

48 Minutes for Palestine toured extensively and internationally between 2010 and 2017. I wrote the script with an introduction that was published in Anna Furse's edited anthology *Theatre in Pieces: Politics, Poetics and Interdisciplinary Collaboration 1968-2010* (London: Bloomsbury Methuen, 2011). In 2017 we re-worked, developed, and re-cast *48 Minutes for Palestine,* with Iman Auon playing the lead alongside Edward Muallem. We re-named the play *Oranges and Stones.* The re-naming of the play was partly because of the new content. It was also a decision taken collectively to counter the prejudice and resistance we received when trying to get bookings for the show, because of the name 'Palestine' in the title. We were explicitly told on more than one occasion in Britain and the United States of America, by albeit supportive directors and festival programmers, that the show would not be booked because of the word 'Palestine' in the title, even though not a single word was uttered in the play. This makes me even more convinced of the power of a play-without-words but with uncompromising stage pictures. The other political irony is that the re-casting of the lead female role was a decision taken in response to the restrictions to freedom of movement placed on that actor, due to the Israeli occupation. Whatever the name of the play, whoever performs it and wherever it is staged, the meaning is the same: this play shows what it is like to live under occupation. It is an allegory for the relationship between Palestine and Israel, from the perspective of a woman whose home is occupied by a man.

Oranges and Stones premiered at Ashtar Theatre on 6 February 2017 with the following cast:

Iman Auon – SAMAR
Edward Muallem – ISSAC

The play is still touring worldwide.

To book the production, for permission to perform this work, or if you would like photos, a link to the video or the music composed, please contact:

Ashtar Theatre, PO Box 17170, East Jerusalem, 91171.
Tel: +972-2-2980037, 2964348/9 fax: + 972-2-2960326
Email: info@ashtar-theatre.org
Website: http://www.ashtar-theatre.org

Characters

SAMAR
Samar is played by a female adult of any age. She starts the play healthy, fit and physically dynamic. She wears traditional Palestinian farming clothes and a light headscarf, all made of light natural fibres. She can alternatively wear earthy-coloured clothes. The actor plays preferably barefoot or in close-fitting light sandals.

ISSAC
Issac is played by a male adult of any age. He begins the play looking thin, dishevelled and close to death. He wears a dark, dirty, broken-down suit (circa 1940s) that is too big for him now. He wears a waistcoat and vest without a shirt and scuffed black leather shoes and black socks.

Whatever the cultural background of the two performers, it is important that the two could be related – their skin tone and features are similar.

Style of playing
The style of the piece arose from training in and studying several influential theatre forms and approaches to performance that may be useful reference points. These influences include Samuel Beckett's *Act Without Words 1 and 2*; psycho-physical actor training with Phillip Zarrilli, which applies principles and practices of the Indian martial art Kalaripayattu as well as Tai Chi and Yoga; Mind/Body (MB) training with Cindy Cummings that partly draws on the Japanese Butoh form; work on power, pleasure and presence with Emilyn Claid; playing games and exercises from the arsenal of the Theatre of the Oppressed developed by Augusto Boal; as well as lived experiences of the occupation.

Here are a few specific notes we found helpful in rehearsals and performances:

- Be fully in the present when you are performing.

- Ground your feet, heel to toe. The play is about the occupation of land.
- Connect your breath with your eyes, body/mind, emotion and each and every action. Nothing is without breath. Breathe through every moment.
- Let all unnecessary action and attitude fall away. No excess expression is required. Approach each action as a task, attached to a choice. Let go of all you don't need to fulfil the tasks you have to do on stage.
- Do not fidget, do not fuss, be economical with movement. Separate each action out. The audience are reading every tiny move, so keep your action as clear and precise, just as you would with text. This is a play-without-words. It is not quite a dance but it is choreographed action and does require clarity and precision with movement.
- Do not express too much with your face. If you over-express with your face, you leave the audience unsatisfied, expecting and wanting words.
- Do not make unnecessary sounds. If you do, the audience start wondering why you are not speaking. Observe the form.
- Release the tension in your face and your jaw. Let the physical action speak for itself.
- As in acting for film, draw the audience in to you rather than pushing meaning out. Connect internally. Hold it within.
- The emotion must be truthful: no shortcuts, no tricks, no lies.
- Know your character and be detailed. You cannot play a symbol. You can only play a person.
- As you will see, the characters make a series of decisions in the play. However, sometimes they are just reacting to the situation they are facing. I have indicated some decisions in the script, however, so

as not to be too repetitive, the moments of decision-making are for the actors to find.

- It is called a play for a reason – play, play, play! Be playful in rehearsals and playful on stage. The play was devised through games and is structured as a series of games of power, space and control. Keep playing games as you work.
- The 'script' has and can be used as audio description material for audience members who are blind or visually impaired. It has also been particularly powerful when presented to D/deaf audiences. This play is for everyone.

Space

It is possible for the play to be performed in the round, with the audience at two ends or end-on. For the purposes of this script the action will be described as if the play was performed end-on, therefore 'upstage', 'downstage', 'stage left' and 'stage right' will be used to describe positioning.

Laid out upon the black ground is a perfect circle of stones (or small rocks), each substantial in size but only big enough to hold in one hand. The circle is approximately five and a half metres in diameter, with approximately thirty centimetres between each rock. Between each rock are two medium-to-large-size oranges. At the upstage-right diagonal the circle of rocks is interrupted by a large round wicker basket containing oranges. On the diagonal opposite the basket, downstage left, the circle is interrupted by a mound of rocks out of which shoots up a single sunflower (preferably real), about the same height as the knee of the female player, if possible. There are pieces of white chalk hidden in the rocks. Stage left of the rock mound, inside the circle, there is a large glass jug full of clean water. Slightly upstage of the jug there is a beautiful old hand-decorated plate/bowl with a matching mug positioned next to it, with a fruit knife with a wooden handle inside the cup. Slightly further upstage of the plate is an old, chipped and slightly rusty white aluminium bowl with a light coloured cloth of natural fibres inside it. All of the objects can be seen by the audience and nothing should block their reading of the stage picture.

Inside the centre of the circle, exactly centre stage, is a rectangular-shaped rug, slightly longer and wider than the body of the female player, made of natural fibres and colours with similar tones to her costume. The shorter side of the rug faces downstage. At the upstage end of the rug, there is an embroidered pillow, with natural colours. Under the pillow is a hand-made leather-bound notebook and aged pencil. Inside the circle, stage right and on the same line as the mound of rocks, there is a fine old wooden chair, facing inside the circle. On the seat of the chair is another beautifully embroidered cushion, again of natural colours. On the downstage back of the chair hangs a very large old door key, strung on to a piece of black elastic. On the opposite diagonal to the chair, upstage left, inside the circle, on the same line as the basket of oranges, sits an old wooden crate. On top of the wooden crate is an old chess/checkers board, which folds in half and will open to reveal a wooden backgammon board, with black and white wooden backgammon pieces.

Music

There is a piece of music created for every 'scene' of the play and there is hardly a moment without music. The music works to shape the performance, to help keep a sense of timing for the actors, as well as emotionally affecting the audience. Original composition was by Rami Washara. Please contact Ashtar Theatre for access to and permission to use this music. Washara's music is instrumental, created with various percussion and stringed instruments including drums, a flute and an oud. The music has Palestinian and Hebrew influences.

Lighting

If available, lighting can be used in the storytelling to great effect. For purposes of simplicity only significant lighting states are described here.

Action

The 'script' is like a map: not the destination, but a guide. The actions can be adapted slightly to suit the actors' bodies, but keep the basic meanings and overall choreography the same. The piece is around forty-eight minutes in duration, or a little longer depending on how long the audience take to enter.

Upbeat percussive music as the audience enter the space. Warm lighting. SAMAR writes and then gathers oranges…

The audience enter as SAMAR sits comfortably on her rug, on her pillow, with body facing downstage, writing rapidly in her leather-bound book. It is the start of the day. She writes her thoughts.

After a few minutes (still as the audience are entering) SAMAR places her pencil inside her book and her book back under her pillow. She gets up with a small spring in her step.

SAMAR goes downstage left and picks one orange from the circle, closest to the mound of rocks. Standing, she gently squeezes the orange. She smiles.

She holds out her long shirt (skirt or dress) and places the orange inside the cloth, like a bag. She continues to gather one orange from each space between the rocks, travelling from the mound of rocks, (leaving one remaining orange centrally between each rock). She moves dynamically and economically, with one foot inside the circle and one foot outside. When she arrives at the basket, SAMAR topples the oranges from her skirt into the basket. She then continues around the circle, gathering one orange from between each stone and leaving one behind, until she reaches the mound of rocks again. She crosses diagonally back to the basket and topples the remaining oranges into the basket.

A circle of alternate oranges and rocks is left behind.

SAMAR lifts the basket full of oranges and returns to the rug. She takes the pencil and book from under her pillow. She looks at the oranges writes notes about what she will do with them.

MUSIC – SAMAR'S THEME

Once the audience is settled, the music changes to SAMAR's theme, a lyrical piece.

SAMAR places her book back under her pillow on the rug and returns the basket to its place in the circle.

SAMAR picks one orange for herself. She feels it. She smells it, breathing in deeply, she smiles. She throws the orange into the air and catches it, a little celebration. This is the first orange of the season.

She walks over to the plate and knife, downstage right.

SAMAR notices the flower. She looks at it, lovingly and touches it lightly.

SAMAR takes her plate and knife. She kneels and starts to remove the orange peel with her knife. She carefully places the excess orange peel on the mound of rocks, looking at the flower. She might decorate the stem of the flower with the orange peel also.

After peeling, SAMAR places a piece of the orange into her mouth, chews it, tastes it, savours it, swallows, smiling and nodding all the while. The orange is even better than she expected it to be. It is delicious. She returns the remainder of the orange to her plate, saving it for later.

Standing, she takes the aluminium bowl and rinses her hands with water from the jug, over the bowl. She does not waste a drop. She carefully swirls the water around her plate. She pours the remaining water in the plate over the knife and over the root of the flower. She slides her forefinger and thumb down each side of the flat of the blade and flicks the excess water on to the sunflower.

SAMAR places the plate face down on the upstage side of the mound of rocks. She then places the knife in the mound of rocks, handle up.

SAMAR takes the excess water from the bowl and pours it onto the flower. She sets the bowl back in its place.

She swiftly takes the cloth and dries her hands. She crosses to the chair. She goes to clean it and notices the key hanging on the back of the chair. She places the key around her neck and then continues to clean the chair, scrubbing from top to bottom. As she kneels, she briefly places her head on the chair pillow, as if her head is on a lap. She caresses the pillow. Then she stands and beats the dust out of the pillow.

Music fades.

As SAMAR is doing these domestic chores, ISSAC is silently approaching, walking backwards, extremely slowly, from upstage centre. He turns downstage as he nears the circle. SAMAR does not see ISSAC, her back is to him as she beats the pillow.

ISSAC wears a suit that is now too big for him. He carries a heavy battered old 1940s suitcase in his left hand and his body is bent from the weight and the exhaustion of a long, hard journey.

MUSIC – ISSAC'S ARRIVAL

SAMAR turns and slightly jumps back with a breath as she sees ISSAC stepping into the circle. She is slightly off-balance but re-calibrates quickly.

ISSAC sees SAMAR. He is also startled. He takes a slight step back out of the circle, while holding her gaze. He then steps, very slowly, into the circle of oranges and stones. He puts his case down next to him.

SAMAR steps slowly stage left, still looking at him, stops near the jug and bowl.

ISSAC takes a moment to look around the circle. SAMAR takes a moment to gently adjust her clothes.

ISSAC's focus slowly wanders down to the jug.

SAMAR looks at the water jug. She looks at ISSAC.

SAMAR decides.

She places the cloth in the bowl and picks up the jug and the mug. She pauses. She turns towards ISSAC. She walks around the circle upstage left. She pauses before the wooden crate.

SAMAR looks at ISSAC.

ISSAC looks at SAMAR.

Hesitantly, carefully, she pours water into the mug and hands it, over the suitcase, to ISSAC, with a smile.

ISSAC swiftly takes the mug of water and drinks, quickly, leaning back until every last drop is gone.

SAMAR watches ISSAC drink.

ISSAC looks at SAMAR, smiles gratefully and hands her the mug. His eyes turn to the jug of water. He grabs the jug from SAMAR's hands, she resists slightly but loses her grip. ISSAC drinks a greater quantity directly from the jug.

SAMAR watches him briefly then persuasively pulls the jug away from him.

She looks at the remaining water, frowning slightly. She inhales and walks swiftly back towards the mound of rocks, placing the water back down. ISSAC watches SAMAR.

ISSAC slowly picks up his suitcase, surveying the room he places his suitcase down, centre stage right.

ISSAC'S MELANCHOLIC MUSIC – THE SUITCASE

ISSAC kneels down and touches the case. He places his ear to the case, as if to listen to it. SAMAR sinks to the stage left edge of the rug, watching him intently. Still with his head on the case, he flicks the right catch open, the sound startles SAMAR a little. He flicks the left catch. He lowers the case so it is flat on the ground and slowly lifts the lid of the case, gently all in time with the music. SAMAR keeps watching intently.

Slowly, he bends down and pulls a crumpled lady's dress from the case. The dress is long and dark with pretty red flowers on it. ISSAC looks at the dress lovingly, mournfully. Holds it up and then folds it lovingly over his left shoulder and holds it close to him, as if embracing a loved one. He sways gently with the dress while walking it a couple of steps upstage. He sits the dress on the chair.

ISSAC returns to the case. He reaches down and takes out a child's sky-blue woollen cardigan. It has been made dirty. He places the cardigan on the edge of the backgammon board and crate, sleeves outstretched.

ISSAC returns to the case. He takes out a pair of red baby's boots. He places the boots underneath the cardigan. It looks like a child.

SAMAR touches her chest and breathes.

ISSAC returns to the case. He picks out an old family photograph, crumpled and burnt at the edges. He walks slowly towards SAMAR, holding up the photograph so she can see. She rises and takes the photograph, looking at it intently. She returns the photo to him.

He then reaches inside his jacket and takes out a rolled-up document. He gives the document to SAMAR.

He goes and places the photo on the rocks, with the image facing downstage to the audience while she reads unrolls the document and reads it upstage, intently.

The audience cannot see the document, but for information, it is a copy of the Balfour Declaration, which reads:

Foreign Office
November 2nd, 1917

Dear Lord Rothschild,

I have much pleasure in conveying to you. On behalf of His Majesty's Government, the following declaration of sympathy with Jewish Zionist aspirations which has been submitted to, and approved by, the Cabinet

'His Majesty's Government view with favour the establishment in Palestine of a national home for the Jewish people, and will use their best endeavours to facilitate the achievement of this object, it being clearly understood that nothing shall be done which may prejudice the civil and religious rights of existing non-Jewish communities in Palestine or the rights and political status enjoyed by Jews in any other country.'

I should be grateful if you would bring this declaration to the knowledge of the Zionist Federation.

Yours,
Arthur James Balfour'[1]

ISSAC returns to where SAMAR is standing upstage and watches her read the document, over her shoulder.

After reading she frowns, takes a deep breath and slams the document back into ISSAC's outstretched hand.

ISSAC reaches for SAMAR's key. With a quick in-breath and wide eyes, she slips the key under her top, hiding it there.

RHYTHMIC MUSIC – REARRANGING THE SPACE

ISSAC returns more briskly to the case now. He takes out an old carved wooden toy car from the case and 'drives' the car quickly along the ground, from the case round the circle, downstage right towards the mound of rocks, where he parks it.

SAMAR quickly goes and picks up the car and marches to ISSAC's case and throws it back into the case as ISSAC takes out his mug and fork inside and places it next to the basket.

A beat.

They look at each other, they cross each other at a pace. ISSAC walks towards the case as SAMAR walks to the basket.

She picks up his mug and fork and puts it back in the case as he picks out a book. He walks towards the wooden crate, removes the backgammon board, slamming it on the floor, places his book on the crate and moves the crate slightly downstage in the circle.

---

1   Accessible at https://www.jewishvirtuallibrary.org/text-of-the-balfour-declaration

SAMAR immediately picks up the book as ISSAC crosses her briskly, going back to the case to pick out the mug again, placing it back next to the basket as she throws the book back into the suitcase.

They cross each other again as she again takes the mug and fork from next to the basket to put it back in the case.

ISSAC takes yet another book from the case and places it on the wooden crate. He now moves the wooden crate upstage centre as SAMAR throws the mug back in the suitcase and slams it.

The music ends.

THE SUITCASE BATTLE

SAMAR decides.

SAMAR picks up the suitcase, it is heavy. She turns and places it outside the circle, where ISSAC first entered.

ISSAC follows her, steps outside the circle, picks up the case and walks past SAMAR with a slight look, he brings the case back into the circle and places it back in exactly the same spot.

SAMAR picks up the case again, looks at ISSAC and puts it back outside the circle.

ISSAC picks up the case, this time not looking at SAMAR, and places it back inside the circle.

SAMAR picks up the case, more quickly this time. She looks at him and places it back outside, landing the case harder now.

ISSAC goes and picks up the case. This time SAMAR stands inside the circle with her arms and legs outstretched, blocking his way back in.

ISSAC pauses briefly, then lifts the case to push SAMAR out of the way.

SAMAR blocks the case and ISSAC behind it with her hands, body and strength.

ISSAC pushes SAMAR until she is almost out of the opposite end of the circle. SAMAR pushes back hard. They struggle with all their strength. The rug is disrupted. SAMAR turns and pushes with her back. They make a complete circle in the struggle. SAMAR turns and uses her head against the case, ISSAC does the same. They turn another circle, pushing harder still, until SAMAR turns to her side and ISSAC pushes SAMAR off balance with the case, knocking her to the ground, stage left. SAMAR lands in a heap on the floor inside the circle, landing badly on her hand. She winces.

ISSAC looks slightly at SAMAR as she curls up from the ground. Still with the case in his arms, he walks back to the position stage right and places the case back down. He stands again behind the case as SAMAR recovers, tending to her injury.

ISSAC reaches back inside his pocket. SAMAR turns on the floor to look at him. ISSAC takes out the document again. He shakes it in the air, gesturing to her, and places it back in his pocket.

ISSAC looks at SAMAR. He takes off his jacket. She watches him from the floor, cradling her hand.

ISSAC hangs his jacket on the chair. He wears a vest and waistcoat underneath.

SAMAR gets up and picks up the jacket and throws it outside at the point where he entered.

POUNDING MUSIC OF INVASION AND RESISTANCE

Once again, but this time more swiftly, ISSAC takes at the lady's dress, the child's cardigan, the child's boots and the car (all his things if he can manage it) from the case whilst SAMAR almost simultaneously takes his things and throws them outside the circle, on a pile with the jacket, upstage centre.

She finally boldly stands on the case, facing stage left, facing ISSAC. He pushes her off the case. She lands on the floor again. She throws her bed pillow at him. He throws it back at her. She holds the pillow to her body and thinks about what to do next.

Meanwhile ISSAC slowly gathers his things outside the circle, with his back facing downstage. Piling his things together.

Meanwhile, SAMAR frantically re-orders her home. She straightens the rug. She cleans the mug with her cloth, wincing slightly as she uses her injured hand. She cleans the backgammon board. She throws the cloth back in the bowl.

She picks up the crate with the backgammon board. She places it upstage centre of the rug. She sits behind the crate and board, facing downstage. She opens the board and starts to set up the backgammon pieces to play the game with herself. She shakes the dice. Thinking. Distressed. She looks at the case. It is still there. ISSAC is still outside the circle.

THINKING MUSIC – ISSAC'S RETURN, THE GAME

Music.

ISSAC slowly turns around, facing inside the circle.

He stands, very still, outside the circle, but right behind her.

ISSAC slowly walks around the circle as SAMAR plays, holding his things closely to his body. He then steps back inside the circle by the rocks.

Music fades out.

SAMAR watches ISSAC as he crosses in front of her.

ISSAC carefully places his things back in the case. SAMAR watches him. Is he leaving?

He closes the suitcase and stands, looking at SAMAR. She is still. He then walks across, and kneels in front of her at the crate and board, with his back facing downstage. He is looking at her. Ready to play the game.

SAMAR picks up the crate and board, stands and moves with it, as far downstage centre inside the circle as she can. She places the crate and board in the other direction this time, facing stage right. ISSAC is still kneeling in the same position upstage with his back to us, even though she has moved.

SAMAR shakes the dice, throws them on the board and begins to play backgammon with herself.

Meanwhile, ISSAC gets up and stands by his suitcase, watching SAMAR. She continues to play, avoiding looking at him.

ISSAC opens his suitcase. He takes out a small black velvet pouch. Remaining by the suitcase he shakes the pouch in the air. It makes a sound.

SAMAR ignores the sound. She continues playing, slamming the backgammon pieces down on the board.

ISSAC walks round the case and chair and stands in front of SAMAR and the board. She continues to play, throwing the dice, moving her own and the opponent's pieces.

ISSAC bends down. He takes one of her pieces, slips it swiftly into his pocket. He places two white chess pieces on his side of the backgammon board and three black pieces on her side of the board.

She picks up the dice. She throws them on the board. Then she picks up his chess pieces and on her knees shoves them back into his velvet pouch.

ISSAC looks at the board. Bends down, picks up the two dice, shakes them and then suddenly throws them upstage onto the rug. SAMAR sees the dice land. She looks back at him sharply and then goes to collect the dice.

Meanwhile, ISSAC kneels down by the board, picks it up, and tosses the backgammon pieces up in the air in SAMAR's direction so that they land on the ground. SAMAR turns around suddenly. He turns the board over, chess side up, placing it back down on the wooden crate.

SAMAR steps back, watching him, breathing and looking around the ground. She goes to pick up the backgammon pieces as ISSAC empties his pouch of chess pieces on to the board and begins to set them up on the chessboard.

ISSAC places the chess pieces firmly in place. SAMAR watches. She then takes her backgammon pieces and begins to throw them at the chess pieces one by one, knocking them over. ISSAC does not look at her. He continues placing his chess pieces as SAMAR knocks all over with her backgammon pieces. She kneels and picks up the chessboard and reverses it back over to the backgammon side. He looks at her.

SAMAR goes to place her backgammon pieces back, but ISSAC takes the board and closes it. SAMAR opens the board again sharply. ISSAC closes it more sharply still. SAMAR opens the board. ISSAC closes the board. SAMAR opens the board. ISSAC closes the board. SAMAR opens the board and turns it round so it is open in the opposite direction. ISSAC closes the board. SAMAR turns the board again and opens it. ISSAC closes it. SAMAR opens it. They open and close the board several times, extremely quickly but neatly, until SAMAR finally places both hands on the open board, and up on her knees presses her weight into it. He is on his knees now too. They glare into each other's eyes, facing each other off.

A beat.

They simultaneously scuttle around the ground, quickly picking up their respective pieces, scattered all over the circle. ISSAC places his chess pieces back in his pouch. SAMAR collects her pieces in her hands and puts them back on the board. Both standing, ISSAC slowly throws another chess piece into the board. SAMAR looks at the piece, looks at ISSAC, takes the piece and stands opposite ISSAC looking at him. She coolly throws the piece in the air towards him. He catches it, uncomfortably. She goes to move away but stops as ISSAC reaches in his pocket and reveals one of her backgammon pieces. He waves it in the air, as he did before with the document. ISSAC walks behind the chair and places her backgammon piece inside his suitcase.

ISSAC then takes a book from his suitcase as SAMAR collects the last of her backgammon pieces from the floor and puts them back on the board.

While SAMAR's back is turned, ISSAC goes and lies on the rug, leaning on his elbow and his side, facing downstage. He reads his book. SAMAR notices him but continues to clear away the backgammon board. She places the board and crate back in place, glaring at ISSAC as she passes him. She places the crate down, turns round.

SAMAR looks at ISSAC, then from behind him grabs and closes his book. ISSAC stands up quickly and goes towards her. She throws the book into the suitcase and takes up a place on her rug.

SAMAR kneels by her pillow, takes her notebook and pencil from under her pillow as ISSAC goes over to the suitcase. They look at each other briefly. SAMAR finds a blank page and begins to write. ISSAC watches her from a distance and tries to read her words.

METHODICAL MUSIC – WRITING AND THINKING

SAMAR holds her book close to her upper body. Intermittently she looks at ISSAC, writes, looks at his suitcase, writes, looks around the space, writes, looks at ISSAC and writes...documenting everything that has happened.

ISSAC crosses behind her, still watching. He bends over her shoulder and looks at the writing. He cannot read it. ISSAC then kneels very closely next to SAMAR, on her left. She looks at him. He smiles a wide smile showing all his teeth. She looks sharply back at her book. He continues to look very closely over her shoulder. She continues writing. He rests his head on her shoulder reading her writing. She shoves him away. He moves slightly but continues to look. She shoves him again, this time moving herself further along the rug at the same time. She shoves again and again until she is at the opposite end of the rug. She sits on the rug, to the side now, with her back facing stage left and legs outstretched, taking up as much of the rug as possible. She reaches for the pillow and places it on her lap, using it as a surface from which to write. ISSAC gets up and faces her from the other end of the rug.

SAMAR writes very quickly and intently now, still documenting. ISSAC watches her. SAMAR continues to write until she feels a pain in her writing hand from where she fell earlier. She stops for a brief moment to flex her injured hand at which point ISSAC swiftly grabs the book and rips out a page. She stands quickly as he throws the book back down on the rug.

SAMAR goes to pick up her notebook as ISSAC folds the ripped paper twice and places it in his book, using it as a bookmark.

Meanwhile SAMAR stands, upstage left, and writes on a fresh page.

ISSAC takes his book and goes to stand behind the chair, diagonal to SAMAR, watching her.

ISSAC picks up the cushion and throws it on the floor in front of the chair, at which point SAMAR drops her book on the floor and goes to grab the cushion just before he can place his feet on it. She backs off away with the cushion, now holding it close to her body, with her head down. Meanwhile ISSAC sits on the chair and begins to read.

SAMAR presses herself into the cushion and thinks. She looks at ISSAC.

She puts the pillow down on the rug and picks up her book and pencil again and starts to draw him. Measuring the proportions, from a distance, with her pencil, as an artist might. She stands and looks at him from different angles, sketching him.

He uncomfortably turns his chair, clockwise, facing downstage, and continues to read his book.

ISSAC moves the chair, far downstage centre, inside the circle, putting his back to SAMAR.

SAMAR gives up drawing. She watches him. He reads his book.

SAMAR picks up the cushion and throws it at ISSAC in frustration. The cushion bounces off his head and lands on the floor. Shocked, ISSAC looks over his shoulder towards her. Then, half smiling, he shakes his head and continues reading.

She picks up the cushion instead and starts to hit his back with it, hard. He seems to be enjoying it. Taking her cue from his reaction she drops the cushion and starts to massage him.

MUSIC – MASSAGE

SAMAR massages ISSAC, very hard. She works from his shoulders and neck all the way down his spine. As she works down his vertebrae, he bends forward. She arrives at his tail-bone, digging in. ISSAC is totally bent over with his weight on his toes and slightly lifted off the chair with his head and body hanging over. Suddenly SAMAR shoves his bottom, throwing him off balance, thus finally getting him off her chair. ISSAC falls forward onto the ground.

SAMAR quickly picks up the chair and sprints away, placing it upstage left of the orange basket. He recovers, turning to watch her.

She sits on the chair, planting her feet firmly on the ground and her hands on her thighs. She looks at him, chin up.

ISSAC looks at SAMAR then looks at the rug. He places his book downstage of the rug, sits on the rug, takes off his shoes and socks, folds his socks, places them carefully inside his shoes and puts them neatly at the end of the rug, facing downstage. SAMAR watches him do all this. He then takes a silk eye-mask on elastic from his right pocket, places it over his eyes, leans back and lies on the rug, with his head on the pillow, perfectly relaxed.

Silence. Lights dim.

SAMAR watches ISSAC sleep.

MUSIC – THINKING WHAT TO DO…

SAMAR brings her hands together, leans forward and looks at ISSAC, breathing.

ISSAC is perfectly still.

Still looking at ISSAC, SAMAR slowly gets up. She walks around his body in a clockwise circle, slowly placing each foot carefully on the ground, heel to toe.

ISSAC does not stir.

SAMAR pauses briefly by the mound of rocks. She looks to the knife. She looks back at ISSAC, she carefully picks up the knife. She goes towards him, stands over his head and lowers the knife to his throat. ISSAC stirs. SAMAR jolts backwards. She changes her mind. She returns the knife to the rocks.

She picks up ISSAC's book, flicks through it looking for some evidence of who he is, she takes back her paper, his bookmark, putting I into her pocket.

She goes over to ISSAC's suitcase on tiptoes now, SAMAR moves quickly.

There is silence.

She bends down and, still half-looking at ISSAC, she gently opens the case. She searches, finds his jacket, searches his pockets and hears the jangle of keys.

ISSAC moves at the sound and starts to breath sharply.

SAMAR notices ISSAC's response. She then deliberately turns the keys in her hand, making a sound again. ISSAC gets up, still with his blindfold on, shaking and breathing sharply. SAMAR then jangles the keys in different places in the circle. ISSAC moves nervously towards the sound, still blindfold. SAMAR becomes more playful, jangling the keys at different heights, quietly, more loudly, throwing them on the ground then running to pick them up before ISSAC can get to them. She builds in pace until she is running all over the circle with ISSAC following the sounds, sightless. Finally she throws the keys right outside the circle, on to the floor downstage left.

Lights up sharply.

ISSAC pulls off his blindfold and glares at SAMAR. He recovers his breathing. ISSAC puts the eye-mask back in his pocket, sees the keys and steps outside the circle. He gathers his keys. SAMAR immediately follows him and when he is outside the circle she blocks his return.

ISSAC steps left, SAMAR blocks him, steps right, SAMAR blocks him, looks down and suddenly sees the handle of the knife, sticking out of the mound of rocks.

ISSAC grabs the knife.

Music – a long sharp piercing note from a stringed instrument.

ISSAC holds the knife to SAMAR's throat and walks her backwards. When they are at the centre of the circle, he stops. She stands, almost catatonic, eyes wide open, facing downstage.

THE KNIFE – WITH A SHARP PIERCING SOUND

ISSAC runs the blade of the knife along SAMAR's body, from her throat, down her chest, round her breast, along her right thigh, continuing he walks the blade round her hip, round her bottom, up her back, across her shoulders, across her neck down her arm and fingertips. ISSAC is smiling lightly.

SAMAR's body tenses at his movements. Her breathing is high in her chest.

ISSAC comes away, stands in front and to the side of her at some distance. He holds out the knife, and gestures with it, a telling off gesture, just as he did before with the document and the backgammon piece. He backs off, and bends down to put the knife in the suitcase.

Music ends.

Suddenly SAMAR runs to the mound of rocks, picks one up and goes to throw it at him. However it flies over the back of her head.

ISSAC jumps with fright, breathing in sharply, he ducks behind the open lid of the suitcase for protection.

SAMAR looks at ISSAC. Realising his fear, she goes to throw the rock again but this time deliberately lets it drop on the floor behind her. ISSAC flinches again, protecting inside the suitcase.

She picks the rock up from the ground and laughs. Again she makes to throw the rock at him but instead throws it in the air above her, just moving out of the way before it hits her, releasing a mock cry of fear. She laughs.

SAMAR continues to throw the rock in the air and jump out of the way, fake-screaming, laughing. She then throws the rock in the air catching it and laughing.

ISSAC's body is hidden inside the suitcase. He looks for and finds a piece of chalk and waves it over his head, like waving a white flag.

SAMAR watches this.

He gently stands up, still waving his white chalk.

He gestures towards her with his chalk. She gestures towards him with her stone.

ISSAC looks around stage right and then decides to draw a straight dividing line on the ground with the chalk, from downstage right, about a quarter of the width of the circle, all the way down, along the stage right end of the rug, continuing in a straight line, past the stage right edge of the chair, ending upstage right.

SAMAR watches him do this action.

ISSAC looks around and paces the space behind the line that he has created for himself. SAMAR looks around the space she has left and also paces.

ISSAC places his toes right on the edge of his side on the downstage right end. SAMAR swiftly goes to the other side of the line, standing directly opposite ISSAC.

Standing directly opposite ISSAC, SAMAR gestures with the stone, in the air, close to ISSAC's face. ISSAC copies her gesture with the chalk in his hand. SAMAR snaps ISSAC's chalk in half.

She surveys the line he has made and the space she has remaining.

She then takes his shoes and throws them, one by one, to ISSAC, to his part of the space. He catches the shoes clumsily and sets them down.

SAMAR then draws around the rug (just three lines to complete the rectangle as one end is already on ISSAC's line).

She then removes the rug, placing it and the pillow next to the crate and game board. She looks at the rectangle shape. She uses this shape as a base from to draw out a large game of hopscotch on the ground. Almost covering the entire space she has left.

Hopscotch ('eks' in Arabic): a pyramid shape drawn on the ground made of three large squares at the bottom, then two squares on top of them, then one square.

SAMAR draws the hopscotch pattern, occasionally looking up at ISSAC who stares at her and the pattern on the ground.

SAMAR puts the chalk on the rock mound. She walks briskly over to the base line and spontaneously gestures with the stone, under arm, towards ISSAC's groin, making a kissing sound with her lips. ISSAC instinctively bends to protect his crotch and back away from her.

SAMAR stands dynamically, with her back to ISSAC, facing the base line of the hopscotch game. Without looking, she coolly kicks the lid of ISSAC's suitcase shut behind her.

PERCUSSIVE RHYTHMS MUSIC FOR THE 'EKS' GAME

SAMAR tosses the stone in her hand, landing it on the top square.

She looks back at ISSAC who looks at her and the game.

SAMAR jumps energetically and skilfully on the squares, feet together, feet apart, crossing her feet, turning around and so on until she lands on the top square with the stone. SAMAR picks up the stone, swirls around and throws the stone into the square closest to the chair, upstage. Again she jumps many squares, on one leg, two legs etc., making her way to the square with the stone. She reaches for the chair and places it into the square where she has landed. She picks up the stone and sits, comfortably on the chair, crossing her legs in a satisfied way, for a moment.

ISSAC watches.

SAMAR continues playing. She throws the stone to the square nearest to her plate and cup. She picks up her plate and cup and places it, like a waitress, in the square with the stone.

She picks up the stone again. She throws it to the downstage right square. She picks up the aluminium bowl behind her. She dances with it briefly on her head. Then she jumps, holding the bowl on her head, setting it down in the square with the stone.

She picks up the stone again. This time she throws the stone (unintentionally) just outside the upstage left square.

Very quickly, ISSAC responds by drawing a new square around SAMAR's rock. He then picks the stone up.

ISSAC looks at SAMAR.

SAMAR looks at ISSAC. SAMAR decides.

She jumps a series of squares, sophisticatedly, dynamically, playfully, until she successfully arrives at the square ISSAC has just drawn. She takes the backgammon board and places it on the new square.

ISSAC throws the stone to an empty space downstage left, by the mound of rocks. ISSAC briskly draws a square around where the stone has landed.

SAMAR jumps from square to square, more artfully and rhythmically now, jumping back and forth, to the side, on one foot etc, until she reaches the new square. She takes an orange from the circle. Throws it in the air, catches it and places it in the new square.

Meanwhile, ISSAC quickly throws the stone outside the circle, far downstage left. ISSAC draws a square around the rock again and picks it up.

SAMAR takes one big jump to the new square, outside the circle, gesturing with both arms in the air, in celebration. Her back is facing downstage.

Music ends.

ISSAC then quickly grabs the cloth and rubs out all of the squares inside the circle, including his line, he is laughing.

SAMAR stamps her feet, her facial muscles tense, she grunts. Frustrated she starts to rub out the square she is standing in with her feet.

When ISSAC has rubbed out all of the squares (there is usually a mess on the ground from where the chalk was, this is good) he goes to the edge of the circle and smiles at SAMAR with arms outstretched. He begins to walk backwards, taking in the whole space with his arms.

SAMAR is breathing heavily.

ISSAC goes to the chair, upstage, looking at SAMAR. He picks up her book, throws it on the ground towards the rocks, and sits on the chair, leaning back, relaxed. He cups his hands on his lap, twirling his thumbs around the other in a thinking/planning gesture while wiggling his toes in a satisfied manner.

SAMAR watches him.

ISSAC leans over to the basket next to him. He selects an orange. He bites into the orange and begins to peel it.

She watches him.

ISSAC takes the bits of peel and throws them on the ground all over the circle.

She watches him.

ISSAC takes a large segment of orange and places it in his mouth. He chews the orange, clearly enjoying the taste. He offers her a piece of orange. She does not move. With raised eyebrows ISSAC looks at SAMAR, cocks his head, then looks at the basket, as if to say 'want one?' He places the remainder of the orange he is eating, into the basket, then picks up a fresh orange and offers it to her in a gesture, similar in movement to the gesture he did before with the document, the backgammon piece and the chalk.

MUSIC – JUGGLING

ISSAC rolls the orange on the ground, towards SAMAR.

SAMAR then marches inside the circle directly towards ISSAC, who stops her by throwing an orange at her.

SAMAR catches the orange.

SAMAR marches towards ISSAC again.

He throws another orange.

SAMAR catches it and heads for him again.

He throws a third orange.

With three oranges in her two hands, SAMAR walks slowly now towards ISSAC.

ISSAC's hand hovers over the basket of oranges, ready to throw another if necessary.

SAMAR pauses in front of the crate, looking sideways at ISSAC.

SAMAR looks at the oranges in her hands, turns away from ISSAC and begins to juggle brilliantly with the oranges, turning a full circle while doing so.

ISSAC removes his hand from the orange basket.

When she arrives back round to face ISSAC, she deliberately drops an orange on the floor. SAMAR stops, drops her head down looking at the fallen orange. With her two hands upwards, she sarcastically shrugs her shoulders.

SAMAR looks at ISSAC, then gestures towards him with the orange in her right hand.

ISSAC closes his body in.

SAMAR then gestures towards herself with the orange in her left hand. She repeats the action. She gestures towards ISSAC with the orange in her right hand a third time and then uses the orange in her right hand to hit the orange in her left hand, three times.

SAMAR decides.

She walks downstage right in the circle and takes a place, feet apart, facing inside the circle.

SAMAR gestures again towards ISSAC with the orange in her right hand. She throws that orange into the air, then swiftly throws the orange in her left hand across to her right hand and back again to her left hand, by the time the orange in the air lands back down into her empty hand. She repeats this juggle, twice.

SAMAR takes a mocking bow, towards ISSAC.

SAMAR crosses diagonally back towards the crate. She gestures to ISSAC with her right hand. She then juggles with the two oranges with her right hand only. One orange follows the other, follows the other... She repeats the motion three times.

Then SAMAR looks towards ISSAC, who is still watching her from the chair.

SAMAR lifts the orange in her right hand into the air. She holds it in her left hand below. She then puppeteers the orange in her left from the orange in her right hand, using an imagined piece of string. At the same time, SAMAR moves her body, puppet-like, towards ISSAC, swaying her head from one side to the other, lifting one leg at a time in a heightened motion, as she gets closer and closer.

ISSAC makes a grab for the oranges but SAMAR quickly moves them out of the way.

SAMAR offers both the oranges to ISSAC.

ISSAC grabs for the oranges again, but SAMAR is too fast. She moves away downstage.

She turns round slowly, putting her back to ISSAC and facing the audience, she looks at the two oranges in her hands.

She thinks.

She looks up.

SAMAR decides.

ISSAC watches her from behind.

MUSIC – SEDUCTION

From downstage centre SAMAR bends over forwards. She places the oranges under her top and on to her own breasts.

SAMAR looks at her now larger breast shape.

She looks straight ahead without expression and raises her arms with palms up.

SAMAR turns around slowly and starts to dance to the music. Looking at ISSAC, she walks the circle, past the rocks, towards the crate and towards ISSAC again and takes him by the hands. ISSAC smiles.

Her hands in his hands, SAMAR seductively pulls ISSAC off her chair. ISSAC smiles. SAMAR looks to her chair, and turns ISSAC round, slowly at first, moving with the music which starts to speed. They move faster and faster until SAMAR is spinning him. On each turn she looks at her chair. She spins him so fast he flies out of the circle, downstage left, towards where she jumped before. ISSAC stands breathing in a broken rhythm.

SAMAR takes the oranges from her breasts and throws them both at him, over arm, violently. He catches them or blocks them so that they do not injure the audience. She grabs the third orange on the ground and slams her arm on to the inside of her elbow, bringing the under arm up (a 'fuck you' gesture), simultaneously casting the orange, under arm, at ISSAC with a long punctuating exhalation as the music ends.

SAMAR backs off, towards her chair, staring at ISSAC.

ISSAC glares at SAMAR. He walks determinedly back in to the circle straight to her.

MUSIC – THE KISS, HEAVY BASE WITH
SHARP PIERCING SOUND

ISSAC moves very in close to SAMAR and grabs the key hanging round her neck. The lighting closes in and is more ominous. SAMAR takes a sharp breath in, pulling away from ISSAC. He continues to pull her, by the key round her neck, back into the centre of the circle. SAMAR focuses on the key. She grabs it, but ISSAC continues to pull. ISSAC then puts his head under the elastic on to which the key is strung. He shoves his knee between SAMAR's legs, grabs her from the back, still pulling tightly. She struggles away, still holding the key. ISSAC slowly leans in, SAMAR struggles, repulsed and desperate and with his full force, he kisses her on the lips. SAMAR gets out of the clinch by pulling the elastic up over her head and letting go of the key. She collapses on to the ground. ISSAC looks at her, looks at the key that is now in his hand and kisses it softly.

SAMAR is crumpled, shaking on the ground.

ISSAC sits on the chair and places the key round his neck.

MUSIC OF SAMAR'S DISTRESS

High pitched sound. SAMAR scrambles, on her knees, over to the bowl. She is downstage slightly to the left of the rock mound. She pours water into the bowl and looks into the water for a brief moment. She then cups the water and scrubs her face, neck, hands and body, with frantic vigour. She pulls off her head-scarf and cleans her hair as well.

ISSAC picks the remainder of his orange from the basket and eats it.

SAMAR is more and more vigorous. The scrubbing becomes scratching – her body, thighs, feet...

ISSAC watches SAMAR as he swallows the last of the orange.

ISSAC decides.

He gets up, crosses the circle, lifts his trousers slightly and steps into SAMAR's water bowl in his bare feet.

SAMAR stops. Mouth and eyes open in shock.

ISSAC stands in the bowl and walks a small circle, splashing the water.

SAMAR watches ISSAC's feet in the water she has used to wash herself.

ISSAC steps out of the bowl, shaking the water off his feet, walks over and dries them on the rug, then continues around the circle back to the chair.

SAMAR looks at the dirty water in the bowl.

ISSAC sits looking at SAMAR.

Silence.

SAMAR suddenly picks up the water bowl and standing, throws the remainder of the dirty water at ISSAC, splashing him in the face as he attempts to get out of the way.

ISSAC glares at SAMAR.

SAMAR looks at the empty bowl from downstage right.

ISSAC crosses the circle towards the rocks as SAMAR backs away, shielding her body with the bowl.

ISSAC looks at the water jug, grabs it. SAMAR looks up at ISSAC with widened eyes.

Looking at SAMAR, ISSAC pours the water over his head as he walks round the circle clockwise.

SAMAR, with short breath, runs towards ISSAC, holding the bowl under his head to try to catch the cascading water. She follows him desperately as he turns circles, shakes his head, wiggles, satisfied, as if in a shower, pouring the water over himself without looking at SAMAR. SAMAR tries to catch every drop of water in the bowl. By the time ISSAC has walked one full circle the water jug is empty.

Arriving back at the rocks, ISSAC pulls the sunflower out of the ground and places the stem, lengthways, into his mouth. He smiles at SAMAR with the stem between his teeth. SAMAR looks at ISSAC. He walks away.

SAMAR looks at the mound of rocks.

ISSAC places the empty jug down on the ground, mid-downstage right, puts the sunflower in the jug and looks at it. He begins to rearrange the objects, establishing a new space.

MUSIC – ISSAC MAKES AN OFFICE

Meanwhile, SAMAR sees water on the ground downstage. She puts the bowl down by the rocks and picks up her cloth. She tries to wipe up all the water over the ground downstage with her cloth. She desperately wrings the cloth out back into the bowl, trying to collect as much of the now sparse water as she can. Her focus is on the task. She does not look at ISSAC. Neither does he look at her.

Meanwhile, ISSAC gets SAMAR's rug and lays it out, centre stage, diagonally. He looks around. He picks up SAMAR's chair. He places it on the rug. He adjusts the cushion. He looks around. He picks up SAMAR's pillow and puts it on the back of the chair. He gets his suitcase and places it in front of the chair. He opens his suitcase and takes out an old typewriter and then a candle. He places the typewriter on the ground, picks up the suitcase and places it in front of the chair, like a desk. ISSAC then places the typewriter on top of the suitcase, at the stage-left end and puts the candle at the other end. ISSAC then takes the jug with sunflower and puts it at the other end of the 'table', next to the candle. ISSAC looks around. He gets the wooden crate with the backgammon board on top. He places the board on the floor to the side of the 'desk'. He places the crate standing up, stage left, like a seat for a visitor to his office. He sees the bowl. While SAMAR is mopping up water, he lifts the bowl, tips out the water SAMAR has gathered and shakes it over the mound of rocks. SAMAR looks at ISSAC. Her mouth falls open.

ISSAC goes to the rock mound and walks swiftly around the inside of the circle, throwing the oranges into the bowl, one by one.

SAMAR is still at first, looking at the ground, then she slowly crawls to the rocks and begins to smash them against one another, looking for water.

When ISSAC gets to the basket, he empties the oranges into it. He continues round the circle, filling the bowl with oranges until they are all collected.

ISSAC places the bowl full of oranges on the downstage-right end of the rug. ISSAC looks at the bowl of oranges.

SAMAR is still smashing rocks. Her injured hand hurts.

ISSAC walks around the back of his newly arranged office area, down to the mound of rocks, and picks up SAMAR's cup. He goes and sits on the chair in his 'office', holding his cup in his right hand close to his face, looking at SAMAR.

SAMAR spreads the mound of rocks. She looks for water beneath it.

SAMAR finds no water under the rocks.

SAMAR sees her book. She sits on the now flat area of rocks and starts to re-read what she wrote before. She reads quickly, her head almost buried in the book.

ISSAC watches SAMAR read, cocking his head to one side.

SAMAR takes out her pencil and writes very quickly, her hand and mind in pain. She grimaces, rocking herself backwards and forwards in distress and self-comfort as she continues to write. She is crying and whimpering.

ISSAC watches SAMAR from his 'office'.

Time passes.

ISSAC decides. He goes over to SAMAR and picks her up. She struggles but she is exhausted. He walks her backwards and sits her on the upturned crate, now a seat. She clutches her book to her body, crying.

He strokes her hair.

She flinches away.

ISSAC takes the pencil and then her book from SAMAR and stands slightly behind her.

SAMAR looks back at ISSAC.

ISSAC puts SAMAR's pencil in the mug, rips several pages out of her book and throws it on the ground. He places several sheets on to the 'table', then sits and rolls a piece of SAMAR's paper into his typewriter.

ISSAC types on SAMAR's words. He types at normal speed at first. Then he notices SAMAR's reaction to the keys being hit. She responds as if each key being hit is hurting her body.

ISSAC watches her. He then starts to slow the typing down, torturing her.

She starts to wail, mouth wide open.

He stops, he looks at her, he picks an orange, he goes to offer it to her but instead shoves the orange into her mouth, blocking out her sound.

She holds the orange in her mouth for a moment then drops it to the ground. Her body follows the orange down to the ground.

She finds some chalk from the rock mound and begins to write on the ground, downstage.

With difficulty, her wrist in pain from the earlier injury, she writes, 'Help', in Arabic, on the floor, diagonally, downstage right.

BUILDING THE WALL – BIG AND BRUTAL MUSIC

ISSAC stands. He takes each and every object from his 'office', all of the objects on stage and places them on top of SAMAR's words. He is constructing a wall with the objects, diagonally, from downstage right to left, leaving SAMAR confined to a small downstage left zone.

She draws all of the things that were once in her home – the water jug, the oranges, the chair etc.

Meanwhile ISSAC continues constructing the wall. He places the wooden crate next to the backgammon board, the jug and flower next to the bowl, the candle in the middle of the suitcase, the chair (with cushions) on its side next to the suitcase, and throws the rug over the chair. Finally ISSAC takes an old lighter from his pocket and lights the candle.

SAMAR looks at her drawing and writing. She has covered the ground: there is nowhere left to mark.

ISSAC stands behind the suitcase, behind the 'wall'. He looks at SAMAR.

SAMAR looks at ISSAC.

There is silence.

ISSAC smiles and then reaches his hand across the 'wall' to shake hands.

SAMAR looks at ISSAC's hand.

SAMAR picks up the candle. She decides. She extinguishes the candle on the palm of ISSAC's hand.

ISSAC relights the candle again. Not looking at SAMAR, he folds his hands on to his stomach, closes his eyes, turns round, and with his back to SAMAR and the 'wall', he starts to sway, backwards and forwards.

SAMAR picks up an orange, facing us, in rage, she rips the orange into two pieces, holding each piece in her outstretched hands.

With a loud yelling sound SAMAR throws the oranges at ISSAC's back and pushes the suitcase, hitting the back of his knees so he falls forward. He turns round, wide-eyed.

SAMAR grabs orange after orange from the remains of the 'wall' and throws them, one at a time, hard, at the suitcase as ISSAC ducks behind it.

ISSAC pulls the case towards him, takes out his jacket and puts it on. He takes three of the oranges and throws the oranges into his suitcase, closes it, picks it up and stands, looking at SAMAR. She ceases throwing oranges but stands threateningly with one in her hand. It seems as if he is going to leave.

ISSAC slowly crosses through the gap in the wall towards SAMAR. He then walks behind her and uses the case to push her in the back with the case, walking her through the gap in the 'wall'. She resists with less strength than before. He walks her upstage to the point in the circle where he first entered and shoves her out.

He grabs the rug and throws it at her feet.

MUSIC – ISSAC'S CELEBRATION

ISSAC turns back into his space, smiling. He goes into the suitcase and takes out a sparkler firework. He waves the firework in the air as the lights dim a little, dancing to the music, conducting with the firework until it dies and music fades out.

MUSIC – SAMAR'S THEME, FLUTE,
MORE SLOWLY NOW

ISSAC breathes heavily after his dance.

He sits on the suitcase, centre stage.

ISSAC takes SAMAR's book and slowly rips out one page. He starts to make a paper aeroplane with it.

Meanwhile, SAMAR stands with her head down and her back facing the circle. SAMAR picks up the rug, wraps it around her shoulders like a cloak and slowly turns round.

SAMAR walks the exterior of the circle, stage-left side. Heel to toe. She looks inside the circle at the space and at ISSAC, until she arrives at the flattened rocks. From the outside, she steps on to the rocks and stands looking out at the audience.

ISSAC flies his paper aeroplane up and out in the direction of SAMAR and the audience.

SAMAR looks at us.

THE END

A post-show discussion often follows. The audience are asked: what did you see…?

THE INTERROGATION OF SANDRA BLAND

Dedicated to Sandra Bland (1987–2015)
and all of our people who have died in police custody

The Interrogation of Sandra Bland was first performed at The Bush Theatre, London on 24 March 2017 with the following creative team.

Creative Team

WRITER / DRAMATURG MOJISOLA ADEBAYO

DIRECTOR OMAR ELERIAN

ASSISTANT DIRECTOR (COMMUNITY CHORUS)
    MOJISOLA ADEBAYO

PERFORMERS ALL PLAYING SANDRA BLAND
SHEILA ATIM
AKIYA HENRY
JUDITH JACOBS
SAPPHIRE JOY
SARAH NILES
JULIET OKOTIE
INDRA OVÉ
Plus a large community cast of women all playing Sandra Bland.

PERFORMER (PLAYING BRIAN ENCINIA) JOHN LAST

PERFORMER (PLAYING FEMALE OFFICER) RUTH MINKLEY

Background

In June 2016, Simeilia Hodge-Dallaway of Artistic Directors of the Future (ADF) invited me and several other black playwrights to write a fifteen-minute play for the first *Black Lives, Black Words* event in London, at The Bush Theatre. The brief was to respond to the question, 'do black lives matter today?' I felt both overwhelmed and humbled at the gravity of the task. I had no idea where to begin. Then I remembered Sandra Bland, having followed (like so many of us have done) an appalling online trail of humiliations and violations of our African kin, across the Atlantic and on our own European island, Britain. I remembered how awed I was by Sandra Bland during the roadside interrogation that lead to her brutal arrest and eventual death by hanging in police custody, recorded on the dashboard camera of the police car that pulled her over. I was moved by Sandra Bland's courage, her wit, intelligence, integrity, strength, tenacity and helplessness in the face of the arresting police officer. The interrogation also struck me as a horribly gripping and dramatic 'scene' that escalates with devastating dramaturgical effect. I thought I could not write anything more compelling or important than this. I could not write anything that demonstrates more acutely the various levels of anti-black racism and white supremacist mentality in action than this. However, I did not want to just re-stage the real-life scene. Anyone can click on YouTube to see it. I have no taste for verbatim plays that only translate reality rather than transport the audience imaginatively. I want theatre to do something that a web page, a news clip or a mainstream documentary cannot do. Then an idea came to me. Let us take the words of Sandra Bland and have them spoken by one hundred black women who all play her. Sandra Bland was evidently a brilliant woman; she was sharp, clever, funny, brave, dignified, talented and educated. There was no one like her and her life can never be replaced. Yet any one of us black women could have been in Sandra Bland's shoes. My idea in having Sandra Bland played by a huge chorus of black women is that she is shown as an every-black-woman. We elevate Sandra Bland's status and the status of all black people who have faced similar situations, through the amplification of the voice, a magnification of the struggle. The performance is in this way a theatrical memorial to Sandra Bland and whom she represents. This is a spoken requiem. Furthermore, by magnifying and illuminating the encounter, audiences are encouraged to investigate the scene and interrogate the interrogation. Lastly, in this performance I want to offer an opportunity for a civic ritual through which as many of us as possible can creatively participate in the Black Lives Matter movement. So I sat down at my desk, watched the online clip over and again and transcribed the roadside interrogation and arrest of Sandra Bland by State Trooper Brian Encinia on the 10 July 2015, in Waller County, Texas, USA.

We chose not to stage the piece as planned in 2016 as the legal proceedings were still in process. Moreover, I really wanted Sandra Bland's family to give us their blessing for the performance to go ahead. We tried, but ADF were not able to reach the family. This raises a question about the ethics of going ahead with the staging; for me, however, this question was answered by the fact that Sandra Bland was herself an active part of the Black Lives Matter movement. For example, she regularly addressed and encouraged her 'Kings and Queens' in her online broadcasts *Sandy Speaks*, speaking to issues of racism and uplifting people who listened. Importantly, Bland specifically called to a passer-by filming her arrest, 'Thank you for recording! Thank you.' Lastly, the dash cam recording is already in the public domain. I hoped that, as we approached the first staging of *The Interrogation of Sandra Bland* at The Bush Theatre on 24 March 2017, we had, in some way, Sandra Bland's own spiritual and political blessing for her unaltered recorded words to be heard and multiplied, loud and clear, with full emotional commitment, in the theatre. If it was me, I would want people to know what happened and how. This was another way of recording and hopefully making something beautiful out of the brutal; something revolutionary out of the revolting abuse of life. Sandra Bland was arrested when she was on her own and she died in a police cell. The amplification of her voice in the staging becomes a collective gesture of solidarity and support. We said to ourselves: Sandra Bland's voice will not be alone again.

The first performances at The Bush Theatre were astonishing. I have worked in theatre for twenty-five years, but I have never experienced anything so powerful. I was shaking. There was a core cast of seven professional black women actors, two white actors playing the police officers, and a huge community cast of women from all cultural backgrounds. The actors, community participants and audience members were deeply moved. There was stunned silence at first and then passionate discussion about the work late into the evening. People are still talking about it. All the actors have kept in touch and still have a deep bond over this work. We felt we had done the right thing in going ahead. I have since used the script with students, conference delegates and participants at community and arts events, where the effect has also been very powerfully, moving and politically galvanizing. We know it works.

Later in 2017, on a trip to work with Dr Ama S. Wray at the University of Wisconsin-Madison, USA, I took a diversion to Chicago and was finally able to meet with one of Sandra Bland's precious sisters, my shero, my Queen, Shante Needham. Our introduction was facilitated by the family lawyer Cannon Lambert, to whom I am also sincerely grateful. I was and am so immensely blessed and touched that Shante Needham gave her blessing for the work, after speaking with and on behalf of the family. Thank you all.

We subsequently presented the first US performance of *The Interrogation of Sandra Bland* as part of the *Black Lives, Black Words, I AM... Fest*, curated and directed by the extraordinary Simeilia Hodge-Dallaway and Reginald Edmund, at Goodman Theatre, Chicago on 29 April 2019. The performance was astonishing. A few days later, new evidence was released about Sandra Bland's unjust arrest. It was as if Simeilia and the huge chorus of women in Chicago had summoned up the truth. The fight for justice continues, and so does the life of this play. We will keep on playing, all over the world, until this systemic violence against our people is merely a shameful chapter in history.

I want to extend my huge thanks to all of you who have made and will make this performance happen so powerfully and beautifully. Thank you to the family of Sandra Bland. Thank you to all who have supported this project in every way. Moreover, thank you to our Queen, Sandra Bland.

How to stage the play

It is crucial that Sandra Bland is played by a large cast of (preferably one hundred) women, lead by black women. I suggest a core group of seven black female professional actors (indicated below as BLAND CORE) plus a large community chorus of culturally diverse women (indicated below as ALL) to play Sandra Bland, plus a white male actor and female actor playing the police officers. This is the concept. In doing this work, on a large scale, but in detail, we are both magnifying Sandra Bland and putting the arrest under a magnifying glass. It must be both a requiem and an uprising, art and activism, a memorial to move the Black Lives Matter movement.

I suggest that the BLAND CORE cast of seven rehearse for one week or more, whatever is possible. The BLAND CORE group of seven can then be joined by the large community chorus of culturally diverse women for shorter periods of rehearsal. At The Bush Theatre in 2017 we rehearsed the chorus for one day. They arrived in the morning, rehearsed with the professional actors all day and then performed in the evening. No one had a script in hand. It is also possible to play the piece without any rehearsal, by projecting the text on a screen, casting it quickly and reading aloud together. This can also be very powerful.

As you will see from the script, some lines are spoken collectively en masse, some lines are taken by one woman, some in pairs, groups and so on. I have suggested numerically where Sandra Bland's lines may be spoken by a solo member of the core (e.g. BLAND ONE), a pair from the core, a grouping or the entire core of seven – indicated by BLAND CORE. ALL means the core plus the community chorus.

Important: unless it says pause, don't. Be tight on cue in Bland's lines: they flow from one mind. Pay attention to Sandra Bland's own striking use of repetition, a kind of call-and-response. This performance is like playing music through words; you have to feel it, you have to listen, deeply. The audience, too, should feel like participants, not mere witnesses, and this sense can guide the quality of playing. Whatever you do, this piece cannot be reduced to a naturalistic staging by three people behind a fourth wall, as that would miss the point entirely. Sandra Bland must be amplified, elevated and magnified, for the reasons I discuss above. There is power in the collective. The words of Encinia, however, are to be spoken by one solitary white male actor, present on stage. He stands behind a microphone on a stand. His voice is the only one that is amplified. There is also a brief exchange with an unnamed female police officer, which should be played by just one white female actor, also physically present, behind a microphone. The piece is technically simple otherwise. There is just a short projection of a statement before and after the performance.

In terms of the actors' playing style, this is a study, an interrogation of an interrogation. As such the text should be spoken with absolute clarity and precision, observing punctuation, including exclamation and question marks. Do not drop a line. The audience must not miss a word unless it is deliberately inaudible. However, there is no need for emotional detachment. Everyone is playing a person. You cannot act a symbol or a function. This is not reading the news; work out what is happening emotionally to the characters and commit to it. It is not, in my opinion, necessary to 'put on' North American accents, unless it feels right to the actors themselves. What is more important is a sense of the African Diasporic rhythm and tone that Sandra Bland displays, black musicality in speech, whether this has African-American, Caribbean, African or Black British flavours, to me this does not matter. It is important to the inclusive ethic of the work that people who are D/deaf or hearing impaired are not excluded from the performance, as performers and spectators. Therefore integration of sign languages, sign language interpretation and or surtitles is encouraged.

The use of / in a line indicates where the next speaking character should inter-cut with their line and dialogue overlaps. BLAND always counts as *one* character. Overlaps are crucial. Pauses should be observed. It might be of interest to explore stylized movement at points and the use and exchange of looks could be key, but whatever movement there is, like all of the staging, should be kept extremely simple and clear. Do not act out the violence literally. There is no need. Let the words do the work.

Projection on screen:

The Interrogation of Sandra Bland
Dedicated to Sandra Bland (1987–2015)
and all our people who have died in police custody

ENCINIA: Hello ma'am.

BLAND CORE: Hi…

ENCINIA: We're the Texas Highway Patrol and the reason for your stop is because you didn't fail… You failed to signal the lane change. You got your driver's license and insurance with you? *(Beat.)* What's wrong?

BLAND ONE: *(Faintly.)* Nothing's wrong.

Pause of around twenty seconds as he looks at the documents.

ENCINIA: How long have you been in Texas?

BLAND TWO: Just got here yesterday.

ENCINIA: Okay. *(Pause.)* Do you have a driver's license?

BLAND THREE: Didn't I give you my driver's license?

ENCINIA: No ma'am. *(BLAND THREE says something inaudible.)* Okay. *(Pause.)* Okay. Where you headed to now?

BLAND THREE says something casual but inaudible.

ENCINIA: Okay. You give me a few minutes all right?

BLAND FOUR: All right.

Long pause of approximately five minutes as OFFICER ENCINIA goes away and keeps SANDRA BLAND waiting in her car. Everybody waits and waits… The tension builds during this waiting time. Then he approaches BLAND again.

ENCINIA: Okay, ma'am. *(Pause.)* You okay?

BLAND FIVE: I'm waiting on you

BLAND CORE: You…

BLAND FIVE: This is your job.

BLAND CORE: I'm waiting on you.

BLAND FIVE: When're you going / to let me go?

ENCINIA: I don't know, you seem very irritated.

BLAND SIX: I am.

BLAND SIX AND SEVEN: I really am.

BLAND SIX: 'Cause I feel like it's crap what I'm getting a ticket for.

BLAND SEVEN: I was getting out of your way.

BLAND ONE: You were speeding up, tailing me, so I move over and you stop me.

BLAND TWO: So yeah, I am a little irritated, but that doesn't stop you from giving me a ticket, so – *(Inaudible.)*

BLAND CORE: – ticket.

ENCINIA: Are you done?

BLAND THREE: You asked me what was wrong and I told you.

ENCINIA: Okay.

BLAND FOUR: So now I'm done, yeah.

ENCINIA: Okay. You mind putting out your cigarette, please? If you don't mind?

BLAND FIVE: I'm in my car why do I have to put out my cigarette?

ENCINIA: Well you can step on out now.

BLAND SIX: I don't have to step out of my car.

ENCINIA: Step out of the car.

BLAND SEVEN: Why am I…

ENCINIA: Step out of the car!

BLAND SEVEN: No.

ALL: No.

BLAND SEVEN: You don't have the right.

ENCINIA: Step / out of the car!

ALL: You do not have the right to do that…

ENCINIA: I do have the right now step out / or I will remove you.

ALL: I refuse to say –

BLAND ONE: I refuse to talk to you other than to identify myself / I am getting removed for a failure to signal?

ENCINIA: Step out or I will remove you. Step out or I will remove you. I'm giving you a lawful order. Get out of the car now, or I'm gonna remove you.

BLAND TWO: And I'm calling my lawyer.

ENCINIA: I'm going to yank you out of here. *(Reaches inside the car.)*

BLAND THREE: Okay, you're going to yank me out of my car?

ENCINIA: Get out.

BLAND FOUR: Okay, alright.

ENCINIA: *(Calling in backup.)* 25-47.

ALL: Let's do this.

ENCINIA: Yeah, we're going to. *(Grabs for BLAND.)*

BLAND FIVE: Don't touch me!

ENCINIA: Get out of the car!

BLAND FIVE, SIX & SEVEN: Don't touch me.

ALL: Don't touch me!

BLAND SEVEN: I'm not under arrest – you don't have the right to / take me out of the car.

ENCINIA: You are under arrest!

BLAND ONE: I'm under arrest?

BLAND TWO: / For what?

BLAND THREE: For what?

BLAND FOUR: For what?

ENCINIA: *(To dispatch.)* 25-47 County FM 10-98. *(Inaudible.)* Send me another unit. *(To BLAND.)* Get out of the car! Get out of the car – now!

BLAND FIVE: Why am I being apprehended? You're trying to give me a ticket / for failure...

ENCINIA: I said get out of the car!

ALL: Why am I being apprehended?

BLAND SIX: / You just opened my car

BLAND CORE: You just opened my car door...

ENCINIA: I'm giving you a lawful order. I'm going to drag you out of here.

BLAND SEVEN: So you're gon', you're threatening to drag me out of my own car?

ENCINIA: GET OUT OF THE CAR!

BLAND ONE: And then you're gonna / stun me?

ENCINIA: *(Slow this line right down, non-naturalistically, like slow-motion.)* **I will light you up!** *(As normal.)* Get out!

BLAND TWO, THREE & FOUR: Wow.

ENCINIA: Now! *(Pointing stun gun at BLAND.)*

BLAND FIVE, SIX & SEVEN: Wow.

ALL: Wow. *(BLAND exits car.)*

ENCINIA: Get out of the car!

BLAND ONE: For a failure to signal?

BLAND TWO & THREE: You're doing all of this / for a failure to signal?

ENCINIA: Get over there.

BLAND FOUR & FIVE: Right. Yeah, yeah, let's take this to court / let's do this.

ENCINIA: Go ahead.

BLAND SIX: For a failure to signal?

ALL: Yep, for a failure to signal!

ENCINIA: Get off the phone! / Get off the phone!

BLAND SEVEN: I'm not on the phone. / I have a right to record. This is my property.

ENCINIA: Put your phone down. Put your phone down!

BLAND CORE: This is my property.

BLAND ONE: Sir?

ENCINIA: Put your phone down, right now! Put your phone down!

BLAND slams phone down on her trunk.

BLAND TWO: For a fucking failure to signal. My goodness. / Y'all are interesting.

ALL: Very interesting.

ENCINIA: Come over here. Come over here now.

BLAND FOUR: You feelin' good about yourself?

ENCINIA: Stand right here. / Stand right there.

BLAND FIVE: You feelin' good about yourself? For a failure to signal?

BLAND FIVE & SIX: You feel real good about yourself don't you?

ALL: You feel good about yourself don't you?

ENCINIA: Turn around. Turn around. Turn around now. / Put your hands behind your back and turn around.

BLAND SEVEN: What, what, why am I being arrested?

ENCINIA: Turn around…

BLAND ONE: Why can't you… Can you tell me why…

ENCINIA: I'm giving you a lawful order. I will tell you.

ALL: Why am I being arrested?

ENCINIA: Turn around!

BLAND TWO: Why won't you tell me that part?

ENCINIA: I'm giving you a lawful order. Turn around…

BLAND THREE: Why will you not tell me / what's going on?

ENCINIA: You are not complying.

BLAND FOUR: I'm not complying 'cause you just pulled me out of my car!

ENCINIA: Turn around!

BLAND FIVE: Are you fucking kidding me? This is some bull… / You know it is!

ENCINIA: Put your hands behind your back.

BLAND SIX: 'Cause you know this is straight bullshit. And you're full of shit!

ALL: Full of straight shit!

BLAND SIX: That's all y'all are is some straight scaredy fucking cops. South Carolina got y'all bitch asses scared. That's all it is.

ALL: Fucking scared of a female.

ENCINIA: If you would've just listened.

BLAND SEVEN: I was trying to sign the fucking ticket –

ALL: – whatever.

ENCINIA: Stop moving!

BLAND ONE: Are you fucking serious?

ENCINIA: Stop moving!

BLAND TWO: Oh I can't wait 'til we go to court.

BLAND TWO, THREE & FOUR: Oooh I can't wait.

BLAND TWO, THREE, FOUR, FIVE & SIX: I cannot wait 'til we go to court.

BLAND CORE: I can't waaait!

ALL: Ooooh I can't wait!

BLAND SIX: You want me to sit down now?

ENCINIA: No.

BLAND SEVEN: Or are you going to throw me to the floor? That would make you feel better about yourself?

ENCINIA: Knock it off!

BLAND ONE: Nah that would make you feel better about yourself?

BLAND TWO: That would make you feel real good wouldn't it?

BLAND THREE: Pussy ass.

BLAND ONE, TWO & THREE: Fucking pussy.

BLAND FOUR: For a failure to signal you're doing all of this. In little ass Prairie View Texas. My God they, they must have…

ENCINIA: You were getting a warning until now you're going to jail.

BLAND FIVE: I'm getting a – for what?

BLAND FIVE & SIX: For what?

ENCINIA: You can come read.

BLAND SIX: I'm getting a warning for what?

ALL: For what!?

ENCINIA: Stay right here.

BLAND SEVEN: Well you just pointed me over there!

ENCINIA: I said stay right there.

BLAND ONE: Get your fucking mind right. Ooh I swear on my life, y'all are some pussies.

BLAND TWO: A pussy-ass cop, for a fucking signal / you're gonna take me to jail.

BLAND THREE: What a pussy!

BLAND CORE: What a pussy... What a p–

ENCINIA: *(Either to dispatch, or the officer arriving on scene.)* I got her in control she's in some handcuffs.

BLAND FOUR: You're about to break my fucking wrist!

ENCINIA: Stop moving.

BLAND FIVE: I'm standing still! You keep moving me –

ALL: – goddammit!

ENCINIA: Stay right here. Stand right there.

BLAND SIX: Don't touch me. Fucking pussy – for a traffic ticket. Doing all this bullshit...

ALL: For a traffic ticket... *(Short pause then door slams.)*

ENCINIA: Come read right over here. This right here says 'a warning'. You started creating the problems.

BLAND SEVEN: You asked me what was wrong! / I'm trying to tell you –

ENCINIA: Do you have anything on your person that's illegal?

BLAND ONE: Do I feel like I got anything on me? This a fucking maxi dress.

ENCINIA: I'm gonna remove your, I'm gonna remove your glasses.

BLAND CORE: This a maxi dress. *(Inaudible.)*

ENCINIA: Come on over here.

BLAND TWO: Fucking asshole. For a – you about to break my wrist. Can you stop?! You're about to fucking break my wrist!

ALL: *(Stretching the word loudly.)* STOP!!!

ENCINIA: Stop moving! Stop now! Stop it!

ALL squeal in pain.

FEMALE OFFICER: Stop resisting ma'am.

ENCINIA: If you would stop then I would tell you!

BLAND THREE: *(Crying.)* For a fucking traffic ticket…

ENCINIA: Now stop!

BLAND FOUR: *(Crying.)* You are such a pussy.

BLAND THREE & FOUR: You are such a pussy.

FEMALE OFFICER: No, you are! / You should not be fighting.

BLAND FIVE AND SIX: *(Crying.)* For a fucking traffic signal!

BLAND CORE: For a traffic signal.

ALL: For a traffic signal.

ENCINIA: You are yanking around. You are yanking around, when you pull away from me / you're resisting arrest.

BLAND SEVEN: *(Crying.)* This make you feel real good don't it.

ALL: It make you feel real good don't it?

BLAND SEVEN: A female for a traffic ticket, / for a traffic ticket.

BLAND ONE: Don't it make you feel good Officer Encinia?

BLAND TWO: I know it make you feel real good.

BLAND THREE: You're a real man now.

BLAND FOUR: You just slammed me, knocked my head into the ground.

BLAND FIVE: I got epilepsy, you motherfucker!

FEMALE OFFICER: *(Faintly.)* I got it. I got it. *(To ENCINIA.)* Take care of yourself.

ENCINIA: *(Spoken immediately after BLAND's 'I got epilepsy, you motherfucker!')* Good. Good.

BLAND SIX & SEVEN: Good? / Good?!

FEMALE OFFICER: / You should have thought about it before you started resisting.

BLAND ONE: All right, all right, this is real good. Real good for a female, yeah. Y'all strong.

ALL: Y'all real strong. Y'all real strong.

ENCINIA: I want you to wait right here. Wait right here.

BLAND TWO: I can't go anywhere with your fucking knee in my back, duh!

ENCINIA: I'm gon' open your door.

FEMALE OFFICER: Okay.

ENCINIA: *(Pause, then to a bystander.)* You need to leave! You need to leave! You need to leave!

Time passes. BLAND continues crying, ALL repeating, 'for a traffic signal, full of shit, really? Really for a traffic signal?' etc, but much of it is inaudible.

ENCINIA: For a warning, for a warning you're going to jail...

BLAND THREE: Whatever

BLAND THREE & FOUR: whatever

BLAND FIVE & SIX: whatever…

ENCINIA: For resisting arrest. Stand up.

BLAND SIX: If I could / I can't.

ENCINIA: Okay, roll over.

ALL: I can't even fucking feel my arms!

ENCINIA: Tuck your knee in, tuck your knee in.

BLAND SEVEN: *(Crying.)* Goddamn. I can't. *(Muffled.)*

ENCINIA: Listen, listen: you're going to sit up on your butt.

BLAND ONE: *(Crying.)* You just slammed my head into the ground and / you do not even care about that.

ALL: I can't even hear!

Both officers simultaneously:

ENCINIA: Sit up on your butt.

FEMALE OFFICER: Listen to how he is telling you to get up. Yes you can.

BLAND THREE: *(Crying.)* He slammed my fucking head into the ground.

ENCINIA: Sit up on your butt. Sit up on your butt.

BLAND FOUR: *(Crying.)* What the hell?

ENCINIA: Now stand up.

BLAND FIVE: *(Crying.)* All of this for a traffic signal. I swear to God.

BLAND SIX: All of this for a traffic signal. *(Clearly to a bystander recording on their mobile phone.)*

ALL: Thank you for recording!

BLAND CORE: Thank you!

BLAND ONE: For a traffic signal – slam me into the ground and everything!

BLAND CORE: Everything!

BLAND ONE: I hope y'all feel good.

ENCINIA: This officer saw everything.

FEMALE OFFICER: I saw everything.

BLAND THREE: I'm so glad to put that – you just got on the scene so whatever.

FEMALE OFFICER: I was…

BLAND FOUR: No you wasn't you were pulling up.

BLAND CORE: No you didn't.

FEMALE OFFICER: No ma'am.

BLAND FIVE: You didn't see everything leading up to it…

FEMALE OFFICER: You know what, I'm not talking to you.

BLAND SIX & SEVEN: You don't have to!

BLAND ONE: You don't have to… *(One by one every woman playing BLAND exits saying, 'You don't have to,' each in their own way. This can be in any language. When the last woman has said it, ENCINIA says his last line.)*

ENCINIA: 25–47 County. Send me a first-available, for arrest.

Projection:

> Three days later, Sandra Bland was found
> hanging in her police cell.

THE END

STARS

A CONCEPT ALBUM FOR THE STAGE

Dedicated to all us survivors

STARS was developed during a residency with idle women in 2016. It was first performed as a staged reading at Ovalhouse Theatre downstairs on 29 June 2018 with the following creative team.

Creative Team

CO-PRODUCER / WRITER / PERFORMER (PLAYING MRS AND ALL CHARACTERS EXCEPT DJ SON) MOJISOLA ADEBAYO

CO-PRODUCER / MUSIC SUPERVISOR AND PRODUCER / DJ PERFORMER (PLAYING DJ SON) DEBO ADEBAYO

DIRECTOR RIKKI BEADLE-BLAIR

DIRECTOR DURING RESEARCH AND DEVELOPMENT PROCESS S. AMA WRAY

ANIMATION ARTIST AND ILLUSTRATOR CANDICE PURWIN

SET AND COSTUME DESIGNER RAJHA SHAKIRY

COSTUME DESIGNER (DURING R&D PROCESS) CLAUDINE ROUSSEAU

LIGHTING DESIGNER PABLO FERNÁNDEZ BAZ

VOICE DIRECTOR ANDREA AINSWORTH

STAGE MANAGER ALISON POTTINGER

CONSULTANT ON INTERSEX VALENTINO VECCHIETTI

CONSULTANT ON FGM RASHA FARAH OF FORWARD

BRITISH SIGN LANGUAGE INTERPRETERS JACQUI BECKFORD, IZEGBUWA OLEGHE

EMERGING ARTIST MENTEES NATALIE COOPER, SONNY (JUNIOR) NWACHUKWU, DIKE OKOH, LETTIE PRECIOUS

ARTISTIC ACCESS WORKERS CONRAD KIRA, KAREN TOMLIN

PRE-SHOW

Music: 'Space is the Place' by Sun Ra. Audience are ideally seated in-the-round or horseshoe to accentuate the storytelling feel. Set not yet fully revealed.

OPENING RITUAL

On house clearance there is silence, haze; a mystical, starry feeling. Enter one male followed by one female performer. He is dressed in robes and a hat that resonate with the culture of Dogon, Mali, as do all the visual elements of the show. He whirs a bullroarer over his head. The humming sound represents the voice of the sacred star, Sirius B/Po Tolo, signifying the arrival of the Nommo. The female performer represents the Nommo – an African androgynous anthro-amphibian space traveller. She is dressed in a costume/headdress/mask inspired by Dogon culture. The two walk slowly, ritualistically, into the ominous dimly lit space. Arriving centre stage, they turn full circle with the bullroarer. Whirring subsides and the two performers are still, facing each other. Lights go black and hand-drawn animation of the Nommo story is projected with voice-over and subtitles (below). All animation in the play connects in some way to MARY/MARYAM, whom we meet later. All words spoken in the play are also projected, either embedded into the animations as subtitles or as surtitles during spoken text, all to support access (especially as music plays throughout the show).

NOMMO ANIMATION/VOICE-OVER: *(Both performers, calling, slow, in sync.)* Nommo… Nommo…

Once we were two

When two was one

Space duo, in solo

We Nommo

Both female and male,

Of land and of sea,

From Po Tolo

Comes Nommo

Of Sirius: B.
Beings of twin
Fish-like-body-persons
With feet and fins
Scales and skin
Rainbow chameleons
Ancestral aliens
This is a tale of tails…

SCENE – THE FUNERAL

During the animation/voice-over the two performers carefully remove their costumes (used again at the end of the show) in the darkness. At the end of the animation, upbeat music (e.g. Hudson Mohawke's 'Scudd Books') kicks in, contrasting the scene. Female performer is now revealed as MRS, our protagonist, a black (or black mixed heritage) woman of around eighty years old. Male performer is her son, a DJ in his thirties. MRS and DJ SON are dressed for a funeral. DJ SON is holding an urn, which he hands to MRS. They embrace, sadly. MRS watches DJ SON walk away. He enters his radio studio, raised and upstage left. He prepares to play a dance music radio set (mixing live) throughout the entire show, no pause. This is a concept album for the stage. Suggestion of a jaded, dated, London council flat kitchen, is revealed downstage right. Significant items: fridge, washing machine, radio, kitchen table (perhaps with a sixties lampshade that looks a little like a spaceship hovering over the table), two chairs. However, the set is non-naturalistic. The play is magic *in its realism. For example, all props that are revealed can come from inside the fridge. MRS goes into her kitchen, places the urn on the table, looks at it – a determined look.*

SCENE – FLASH-FORWARD TO GP

A flash-forward in time. 'Scudd Books' cuts out immediately as we find MRS sitting in the chair of the GP's surgery, down centre stage. She faces the audience. 'Perotation 6' by Floating Points plays. Female performer plays MRS and the GP (and all characters except DJ SON). MRS speaks with a South East London accent. GP is white English RP. All live spoken text is projected in surtitles, displayed from the DJ's radio studio.

MRS: Me husband died
And it's taken my whole life
But Doctor,
I've never had one
And I want one
Before I die.
I want to know what it's like.
What is wrong with me?

GP: Anorgasmia

MRS: She said.
Ain't that a flower?

GP: Also known as 'Coughlan's syndrome'.

MRS: Nice Irish name.

GP: An inability to orgasm. Sometimes because of lack of adequate stimulation, sometimes it's caused by trauma: fight, flight, freeze. Sometimes –

MRS: – sometimes, I feel I almost might, when I have a forbidden thought…and then I…sneeze. Do you think it's connected?

GP: I really don't know about that Mrs…

MRS: Could there be a cure?

GP: Have you ever tried…self-help?

MRS: I had a lavender bath and candles.

GP: I mean, perhaps with an electrical device? Not in the bath of course, that would be dangerous. Was there anything else Mrs… We are past our ten minutes and you are well past menopause so perhaps you'd like to find a hobby instead? And I'd like you to book in for a dementia test – it's just a precaution…

MRS: Dementia?

Hobby!

Electrical device?!

I need to find a *cure*.

My orgasm has got to be out there

Somewhere!

SCENE – KITCHEN

MRS is back in the kitchen looking at the urn on the table as before. There is also a goldfish bowl filled with water (the goldfish is not real), a radio, an ashtray, a packet of cigarettes, a lighter, the newspaper The Mirror, *reading glasses and a mug of tea on the table. MRS sits. Turns on the radio. Sips tea. Listens to DJ SON speaking softly, unassuming, through the mic. MRS proudly mouths his tag line (below): 'Taking you through the night, sci-fi style. Frequencies open.'*

DJ SON: This is Michael Manners, the original AfroCelt on NTX.

MRS: That's my boy…

DJ SON: Show's dedicated to Terry Manners. Taking you through the night, sci-fi style. Frequencies open…

DJ SON plays 'West G Cafeteria' by the Space Dimension Controller. MRS listens, takes out a cigarette, clocks it is the last one in the box, lights it, watching the urn.

MRS: *(Quoting MR, her dead husband.)* 'What now Mrs?' What now… *(Music underscore. MRS sits, takes her reading glasses, opens* The Mirror *newspaper and reads her horoscope.)* 'Planetary activity in Leo, and today's new moon marks the start of a personal adventure – even at the onset of winter. Despite the fact a pursuit of yours turned out to be a flight of fancy, you should accept an invitation from afar, without hesitation. Keep doors open. Breathe new air. Throw caution to the wind'.

(To the fish in the goldfish bowl.) Well Cat, what do we make of that? *(Listens in her mind to Cat, the fish, who she hears saying 'time to give up smoking'.)* Agreed. *(MRS draws deep on her last cigarette. Stubs it out. Takes a deep breath. She might cough. Sips tea. Pauses at a newspaper article.)*

'Government plans to send refugees into space.
Five years after Brexit – Project Spexit: Space exit.'
(Imagining.) Immigrants on Mars...
Asylum on Saturn...
Aliens meet the aliens...
(Reading an advert next to the article.) 'Whether you are an exile or an expat, you can apply for Project Spexit in partnership with the *Virgin* Space Travel Programme. Budget planet relocation (one way) or luxury space holiday (return). Terms and conditions... Apply online now!'

Wow.

'www...'

(Disappointed as she is not online.) Don't no one use pen and paper anymore...

DJ SON: This is Space Dimension Controller with 'West G Cafeteria'.

MRS: Cat food! How rude, I am forgetting myself.

She gets fish food from the fridge. The fridge stores all props. She empties the container of fish flakes. There are only a few flakes left. She feels guilty for neglecting Cat.

Whatchu lookin' at me like that for? Shop's shut. You'll have to wait 'til morning… *(MRS hears Cat suggesting, 'How about a sprinkling of the old man?' MRS reacts shocked.)* I can't do that! *(She hears Cat saying, 'Well he ate fish, didn't he?')*

You're not wrong about that, Cat.
Mr probably finished off several of your relatives,
Beer battered with vinegar and chips,
Licking his lips,
Pissed. *(Picking up the urn, impersonating MR. NB: Here and throughout the play, the performer should embody action that is described, act out the memories, keep it live.)*
Staggering back to manhandle his Mrs every Friday,
Saturday, any day, any night
So –

DJ SON & MRS: *(Simultaneously without awareness of each other.)*
What goes around…

DJ SON: …comes around.

Music. MRS empties the ashes from the urn into the goldfish bowl. The fish gobbles the ashes. MRS laughs.

DJ SON: 'Fight'. This track is one of mine on Native City. Good memories of my old man, Terry.

MRS hears her SON; shame. Then to the audience, her confessors.

MRS: What must you think of me?
(Justifying herself.) Sixty years of 'honour and obey'
I was a zombie, a slave,
The *living* dead, that was me.
He don't feel nothing now do he?
He don't feel nothing at all.
So nothing's changed there.
There's not a husband, a father

Only a jailer.
But I've served my time in this space.
I've known my place.

MRS starts saying the line along with the music, enjoying the freedom.

Yeah I've served my time in this space,
I've known my place.
What *now*?

DJ SON: 'Travlin'' by Norm Talley…

Sound of doorbell. Animation projected: through a spy-hole, on the landing of the council block, we see a girl, MARY, around eleven years old, of African descent, ringing the doorbell, desperate to use the toilet, and MRS letting her in. Animation could become abstract to convey time passing, the moon (symbolising MRS' husband) disappears. The sun (symbolising MARY) rises. Quick change into MRS' comfy indoor clothes.

SCENE – MRS AND MARY BECOME FRIENDS

Another doorbell. MRS is brighter, comfy clothes, slippers, now smoking a vape. MARY is at the door. Female performer plays MRS, MARY and all the characters (except the DJ SON). MARY is polite, confident, innocent, matter-of-fact. She speaks RP English but as a second language, with a faint memory of somewhere in Africa – non-specific.

MRS: Hello again little friend.

MARY: I brought you chocolates, for my birthday. *(Offering a box of Celebrations chocolates.)*

MRS: It's not my birthday.

MARY: I know, that's why I said it, *my* birthday.

MRS: Oh, happy birthday. Aren't you the one supposed to be getting presents?

MARY: I got lots of presents. I got…holiday.

MRS: Oh… Going anywhere nice?

MARY: Been already. Came back for big school starting. Was saving Celebrations but Mum said I should give them to you to say thank you.

MRS: What for?

MARY: Yesterday's toilet.

MRS: Oh right. No need to thank me, just being neighbourly, but…come in and have a Celebration anyway.

They go inside. MRS goes over to the table with MARY, who is scared of the fish.

MRS: Make yourself at home. He's all right, he don't bite. If my furry friend Feena was still alive she'd likely have a scratch but this cat's safe in his bowl.

MARY looks confused. MRS empties a few of the chocolates on the table.

MRS: *(Referring to the chocolates.)* What's your favourite?

MARY: Number three: Galaxy. Number two: Milky Way. Number one: Mars. I love planets and stars.

MRS: You wanna apply for that Spexit.

MARY: Doing a project for school. And when I grow up I am going be a spacewoman.

MRS: Oooh a little Lieutenant Uhura. I always felt a bit like her when I worked at British Telecom. *(Like Uhura.)* 'Hailing frequencies open, Captain.'

MARY: What?

MRS: *Star Trek.*

MARY: No, *Star Trek* not real. I am going to be real, like Mae Jemison.

MRS: Who?

MARY: First black woman up there. But I will be first from my country. *(She points up.)*

MRS: *(Like E.T.)* 'Phone home…'

MARY: Huh?

MRS: *E.T.*

MARY: I don't know what you are talking about.

MRS: *(Like Tom Hanks in* Apollo 13.*)* 'Houston, we have a problem.'

MARY: I know. I need more science.

MRS: You better have a Mars then. I'll put the kettle on.
(To the audience.) And that's how it started.
We finished off the Celebrations
Every afternoon after school
While she worked on her stars project.
Then she'd have a pee and I'd a vape and a cup of tea.

Short animation as MRS picks up MARY's stars project book and flicks through the pages. We briefly see fragments of MARY's drawings, writing, diagrams…

'What are you doing in there Mary…?'
She said she liked the quiet,
She says she liked my toilet,
The woolly loo-roll holder – she reads astronomy.
Feeling sorry for the grieving old lady
She'd fetch me *The Mirror*, daily.

MARY: But *Metro* is free?

MRS: Sometimes you gotta pay for quality Mary.
   Her name ain't even Mary,
   Her name is Maryam
   But no one at school can say it right
   And Mary sounds less Muslim.
   She went to Catholic school see,
   The primary attached to my parish
   And after that soldier got his head chopped off in Woolwich
   It was easier to be a Mary than a Maryam.

   MRS says the rosary several times throughout the play.

   Hail Mary, full of grace
   The Lord is with thee
   Blessed art thee amongst women
   And blessed is the fruit of thy womb, Jesus

DJ SON: Here's Rhythm is Rhythm with 'Strings of Life'…

   SCENE – MEMORIES OF CHURCH AND CHILDREN

MRS: I got born again for ten minutes
   Searching for 'the final frontier'
   When Mr was having his affair with Venus
   (Calling towards flat in the opposite block.) From over there!
   I was lonely and they give you free chicken on a Sunday.
   But Venus eventually had enough of his drinking 'n' pissing
   in the bed so he came back and shat in ours instead
   And I went back to mass.
   I dunno,
   Maybe I needed to believe leaving him was a sin,
   Maybe I'm scared of it:
   Freedom.
   And being Catholic is much more straightforward than
   being a happy clappy,

All those dancing socks-in-sandals –
You know where you stand when you're in Rome

MRS re-plays her time in a born again Christian Church. Goes into the audience.

I could just never fall in the
Evangelical hall,
I've never been very good at being ecstatic.
I look around one revival
And it's like they're all having seizures,
Trembling, heaving and talking in tongues:
'Mymamamazgottasuzukimypapasgottahondamypapasaz
gottasuzukimamamassgottahondaaaaaIwannaHyundaiI
wannaHyundaiIwannaHyundai…'
But I don't go nowhere
I'm just stood there
And no matter how hard the preacher push-push-pushes
(Reaching towards a carefully chosen audience member.)
My head
I just can't let go of my bones.

Returning to the stage/on the bus.

When it's all over I have chips and curry sauce on the
bus back to Woolwich.
My kind of communion.
Chris always waits for me to leave the service
Pretends he's going the same way,
He's one of those hippy holys…

CHRIS: Jesus got me off heroin – hallelujah.

MRS: Praise the Lord.
Church was full of unhappy wives and people with addictions,
Chris gets me talking on the bus about unlikely attractions

How he likes –

CHRIS: – older women and there's nothing against it in The Bible, Old Testament or New…

MRS: And as I dunked my chips in the curry sauce I confessed to him that I – sometimes feel drawn to women and my husband's my biggest regret.
He went silent.
I hadn't a clue it was me Chris had a crush on.
Not very Christ-like
I was fucking forty-four he could have been my son!
(Wistful.) But my son hadn't yet come
I imagined him to be waiting on a star…
And when by some miracle at forty-six I managed to hatch one good egg *(Picking up the radio.)*
And my little boy finally arrived – alive! *(Clutching the radio to her chest.)*
And I squeeeeeeeeze him close to my breast for eighteen years until he says –

DJ SON: *(Suffocated.)* I can't bear it anymore, mum.

MRS: And he leaves me.
To study music at Uni and then spinning his discs around the world… *(Quoting Spock, as if saying goodbye.)* 'Live long and prosper,' son.
He's got his own radio show now, *(She pauses to listen then speaks into the radio as if her SON is tiny.)* Done all right for yourself haven't you my little Mikey…

DJ SON: No one calls me 'Mikey', Mum. *(Quoting his business card.)* Michael Manners: Music Producer. DJ. Broadcaster.

MRS: And I think –
(Sudden rage, directed at her SON.) Weren't it me that ripped
To arsehole from fanny squeezing your big head out of me

Then clawed my way through the menopause with you
screeeeeaming at me?
Weren't it me that worked day and night shifts all them years
to put music in your fingers and ears?
Weren't it me that stood in the way of you and Mr's fist
So you wouldn't know what you had missed?
– I can call you what I like you arrogant little shit!
And then I caught my thought.
Mother Mary forgive me.
'Yes of course: Michael.
Cuppa tea?
Where's my manners?
I forget.'
Yeah, he's done all right for himself Michael,
considering…
Where was I? –

DJ SON: 'Lunar'… track's by Acre.

MRS: Back to the bus with Chris
    Who's half the man my son's grown up to be.
    Prick goes and tells someone giving him 'spiritual
    counselling'
    That he's got an obsession for some kind of… *(Whisper.)*
    Lesbian.
    'Course it goes around the congregation like a bush fire.
    They haul me in to an 'emergency house meeting'
    (Acting out the memory.)
    I have to take a shift off
    Semi-detached in Greenwich
    Ornate iron gate, original tiling,
    I think to myself, now that's a lot of tithing.
    They sit me down at the big oak kitchen table,
    And without so much as a 'howdy-do' or a 'Hallelu–'

Pull down the velux *(pronounced 'velloo')* blinds announcing –

Playing CHURCH ELDERS:

CHURCH ELDER 1: Your body is a temple and you haven't
kept it clean.

CHURCH ELDER 2: That is why your husband treats you

MRS: the way he did.

CHURCH ELDER 3: That's why he turns to other women and drink.

MRS: Even implied that is why my first child

CHURCH ELDER 1: *was* still born…

MRS: My Gabrielle.
My wingless angel,
Who I love, even if they said she was disabled,
Who I love, even though Mr said –

MR: *(Suddenly; cockney.)* She was better off dead.

MRS: The bastard.
Born-agains said my womb

CHURCH ELDER 1: has an omen, Satan has a hold.

CHURCH ELDER 2: That is why you cannot conceive.

CHURCH ELDER 3: Believe-believe-believe.

MRS: And they try to squeeze the

CHURCH ELDER 1: deeemon of lesbianism out-out-out!!!

MRS: Of me. Declaring it

CHURCH ELDER 1: entered in through horoscopes,

CHURCH ELDER 2: sci-fi films

CHURCH ELDER 3: and pagans in your *black* ancestry.

MRS: Out comes a saucepan. *(Re-playing with the goldfish bowl.)*
    'LeCruset' *(pronounced 'le-cru-zay')* no less
    A big heavy orange one
    Very middle-class
    All place their white hands on my black head, shoulders, breasts
    and press-press-press
    And there's me, leaning over the saucepan,
    And there's them, expecting the

CHURCH ELDER 1: EVIL SPIRIT

MRS: to come out in my vomit
    But all I can manage is a little bit of spit.
    (Ironic.) Such a disappointment *(Returns the goldfish bowl.)*
    Never felt quite right with the Evangelicals after that.
    And then when Mr finally pulls his penis out of Venus
    And they all go

CHURCH ELDER 1: Praise be! Our prayers have been answered.

MRS: And I get pregnant with my son and the elders call
    another house meeting

CHURCH ELDER 2: Just in case there's another demon.

MRS: And then that Freddie Mercury from Queen dies
    And the Leader stands up in the Sunday celebration
    and says

CHURCH ELDER 1: Mercury got what he deserved, AIDS,
    the curse –

MRS: I says no.
    Enough!
    None of this sounds like gentle Jesus or Mother Mary to me
    And I love 'Bohemian Rhapsody',

Now Freddie could take you to outer space…

Bohemian Rhapsody' mixes in momentarily with animation from MARY's stars book. MRS flicks through the book, enjoying the music. Mercury's voice rings out: 'Mama…'

SCENE – MARY AND MRS OBSERVE THE NEIGHBOURS

MRS and MARY watch the neighbours from the window. DJ SON mixes in 'Moondance'.

MRS: Mary changed my night to day.

This flat is the deck of the Starship Enterprise.

(Quoting Star Trek.) 'It's life,' Maryam, 'but not as we know it.'

DJ SON: 'Moondance' on Tribe.

MRS: We're watching the whole constellation of the council estate. Surveying the 'neighbouring planets' over the kitchen plates. She talks me through it all while I have a vape.

MARY: The universe accelerates.

MRS: But looks like our estate is going backwards… Look at him, on his phone by the railing, raging. *(Impersonating the young blood from the estate.)* 'It's the system, it's the system…'

MARY: Jupiter. Hot-head. Full of gas. Could have been a star… Look, Neptune is going out. Only after sunset you see him… Dark rings around his eyes.

MRS: Probably working shifts. And look who's coming across the playground.

MARY: Saturn.

MRS: Stunning.

MARY: Big rings in her ears.

MRS: Afro-centric Empress. *(MRS calls.)* Yes my sister! Saturn!

SATURN: Greetings Auntie!

MRS: Auntie? *(MRS is disappointed, realizing how old she appears.)*

MARY: Look, sitting on the bench, Uranus!

MRS: Don't be rude.

MARY: Mrs your jokes are older than you. Uranus looks like his face flipped over. And see, Pluto coming home with her shopping. Pluto's not a real planet. She's a dwarf.

MRS: Don't call her that. She's your height and you wouldn't like it. Gets laughed at but gets on with it. *(Calls out to the woman of short stature passing, with her thumb up.)* Respect! *(The woman looks up.)*

PLUTO: *(A little cynically.)* Hi.

MRS: And look who it ain't. *(Kisses her teeth.)*

MARY: Venus? She is really hot. *(MRS grunts.)* And he is really cold, my favourite.

MRS: Where?

MARY: The homeless man in big winter coat and bright red face. All year round.

MRS: *(Singing, badly, extracts from Bowie's 'Life on Mars'.)*
'Oh man, wonder if he'll ever know
He's in the best selling show
(Calling out of the window.) Is there life on Mars?!'

MARY is laughing and applauding.

MRS: *(To the radio.)* Let's have a bit of Bowie, Mikey!
Those were the days. Just never thought I'd outlive him.

MARY: Your husband?

MRS: No. David Bowie! South London's finest.

MARY: Nah, Stormzy. Much better.

MRS: *(Like Stormzy.)* 'You're getting way too big for your boots.'

They laugh.

MRS: No… I always knew I'd outlive Mr. He was weak.

MARY: But he loved you?

MRS: He might have done. He just didn't know how. Love is
what you do, innit?

DJ SON: I'm playing this one on a promise. Here's 'Falling
Rizlas' from Actress…

They listen to the music for a moment.

MRS: Who am I then?

MARY: Earth.

MRS: Me? Planet Earth? No.

MARY: Yes. You are.

MRS: Why?

MARY: Because you are mostly blue and covered in clouds.

MRS: Oh.

MARY: And Mr, he is like the moon, always following you
around, even though he is dead.

MRS: Blimey.

MARY: And Mrs you are not a healthy planet. *(Pointing to the
vape.)* This is not good for you. I read it in *Metro*.

MRS: Heavens. Anything else Dr Spock?

MARY: *(A joke.)* Dr *who*?

MRS: *(MRS quotes* Dr Who.*)* 'Geronimo!' *(Laughs, conceding defeat to MARY.)* I'm not exactly… 'Mother Earth' then.

MARY: Sorry.

MRS: It's all right. You're probably right. But you, little one, are the sun, brightening up my day.

MARY smiles. Then a sad pause.

MARY: If I am the sun
    Maybe that is why
    I burn.
    If I am the sun,
    Maybe that is why
    If you looked at me
    You would close your eyes…
    Perhaps I will build a rocket
    For my school project
    So I can fly closer
    To myself
    And then I will keep on flying
    (Line sung like acoustic version of Jamila Woods' song.) 'Way up'
    After myself
    To a little star in the dark
    'Po Tolo'/Home
    From where the 'Nommos' come…

DJ SON: 'Bouramsy' from Lil Silva.

NOMMO STORY, PART 1 – ANIMATION INTERLUDE

Animation. MARY is recounting the story of the Nommo to MRS, while she is drawing them for her stars school project. We see the drawings. Text in voice-over/subtitles.

MRS: So, the story goes…

MARY: The Nommos
    Were migrants from across the cosmos
    Sailing the sky to planet Earth.
    Descendants from a star that you and I cannot see –

MRS: With naked eyes at least –

MARY: Sirius B.
    And for thousands of years,
    Sirius A we could see
    But Sirius B was known only
    To the Dogon of Mali.

MRS: Cousins to the Pharaohs?

MARY: Who knows.
    The Dogon call Sirius B 'Po Tolo'.
    'Po'?

MRS: – star!

MARY: Tolo – the tiniest white seed you can scatter in a field

MRS: Yet still grow food for your babies.

MARY: The white scientists could not see this star.

MRS: Nor could the Dogon, it's too small, too far.

MARY: But their fathers were told of Po Tolo
    By?

MRS: – the Nommos!

MARY: Ancestor aliens sailing to Africa in a spaceship from Sirius B.

MRS: Seriously?

MARY: They say Sirius B orbits Sirius A every half of a century…
And Dogon paint all they know of the cosmos from the Nommos
On the walls of houses,
Celebrating with rituals, sculptures, dances!

MRS: Dogon art exhibits in New York-London-Paris
Making Picasso a modernist and careers for anthropologists.

MARY: And then one day
Through a big telescope

MRS: Old blue eyes said
(Impersonating an English SCHOLAR.) 'Indeed
Sirius has a B that cannot – *nakedly* – be seen.'
And he took a photo,

MARY: In 1970.

MRS: European scholars –

MRS as the SCHOLARS:

SCHOLAR 1: What a wonder!
The star really is very, very dense
Just as that remote tribe said
And it is as white as snow…
But how could these old black Africans know?

SCHOLAR 2: Their cave paintings reveal the vastness of the universe!
Before *us* they knew of Jupiter's moons!

And the rings of Saturn – they could see!

And Sirius B *does* orbit Sirius A for fifty years *precisely*.

SCHOLAR 3: They knew that the planets revolve around the sun

And that the Earth was born from a big BIG bang.

While we were still drawing maps of the Earth as flat

And believed the horizon was the end of it.

When we were still too scared to set sail,

For fear our boats would fall off into hell,

When we still believed the sun revolved around *us*

SCHOLAR 2: And the dark creatures of the Earth were wicked primitive savages

SCHOLAR 1: While we were burning witches and heretics

MRS: It seems these Africans were intergalactic!

MARY: The Dogon knew all about Sirius

MRS: How-could-that-be…?

MARY: We told you! We were told by…

MRS: …the Nommos!

Extraterrestrial Afro-hermaphrodite anthro-amphibian migrants!

MARY: Both male and

MRS: female.

MARY: Of land and

MRS: of sea.

MARY: Like humans and

MRS: fish!

MARY: With feet and

MRS: fins!

MARY: Scales and

MRS: skin.

MARY: Ancestor aliens!
    Rainbow chameleons!

MRS: This is a tale of tails…

DJ SON: Toumani Diabate: 'Salaman'.

SCENE – MARYAM'S REVELATION

MRS: She said

MARY: it burnt.

MRS: Like no temperature you could touch,
    When she was cut,
    In the Summer holidays.
    Her eyes clenched shut.
    Hands pressing her head, shoulders, legs…

MARY: It was so painful.

MRS: Shameful.
    But she insisted –

MARY: They did it because they love me.

MRS: Her parents.
    That's why she wouldn't – *(Grabbing her mobile phone.)*
    'Let me phone the police! I should call social services!'

MARY: No! Please Mrs, don't say, they might take me away…

MRS: And I know it's selfish but
   I was afraid they might take her from me too...
   So 'it's our own little secret'.
   Why she liked to use my toilet.
   Why it took her fifteen minutes to pee.
   Why it –

MARY: *(Through pain.)* – stings.

MRS: And she transports herself –

MARY: – to the stars!

   A monologue from MARY, sitting on the toilet, clutching a book called
   STARS *by Andrew King, reciting what she has learnt to distract*
   herself from excruciating pain.

MARY: 'Every atom of your body
   Was once part of a star'.
   Part of a star...
   Part of a star...
   An atom is the smallest matter
   That 'cannot be cut.'[1]
   Cannot be cut.
   Can never be cut
   To the stars you must return,
   Maryam,
   To the stars you must return...

MRS: So that was why she shuffled her feet across the estate
   Why she was losing weight.
   No matter how many Galaxy's she ate.
   She said...

---

1 From Andrew King's, *STARS: A Very Short Introduction* (Oxford: Oxford University Press, 2012), p. 1 and 29.

MARY: *(Recovering from the pain momentarily.)* When you look
    into the stars you look into the past…
    But you can't change it.

MRS: If I could,
    I would…

*DJ SON rewinds the track and plays forward again with 'Bouramsy'
over NOMMO STORY, PART 2 – ANIMATION INTERLUDE.*

Holy Mary, Mother of God
Pray for us sinners now and in the hour of our death…

NOMMO STORY, PART 2 – ANIMATION INTERLUDE

Text is in voice-over/subtitles as with Part 1.

MARY: But,
    Just like Earth and moon are partners in destiny
    Just like Sirius B is one part only of a shining binary
    With Sirius A –

MRS: The Dog Star – man's brightest friend
    This starry story also has a *contradictory* companion:

MARY: The Dogon *also* believe in one God,
    In the sky

MRS: Sounds familiar

MARY: Amma,
    Who wanted the Earth as His celestial… *(Hesitating, shy of
    the subject.)*

MRS: *(Sexual.)* Partner

MARY: But he could not… *(Hesitating.)*

MRS: 'Mount her'

MARY: Because her… *(Hesitating.)*

MRS: 'Mountain' was too big

> *(Aside just for the adult audience.)* It got in the way,
> he couldn't get it in.

MARY: The wilful single mother Earth gave birth
> To a jackal, a devil instead!

MRS: Whom Amma rejects as he could not possibly be the father.

MARY: The devil/jackal runs around bringing the world into
> disorder.
> So Amma created the Nommo as messengers, saviours of
> the world!
> But even though the Nommo are

MRS: transmitters of all the Dogon know,

MARY: to the people, Nommo look… *(Hesitating.)*

MRS: Troubling,
> As doubling androgynes,
> Their bodies ugly and fishy with excessively fleshy
> differing…

MARY: So Dogon believe to stop the world from all this disorder

MRS: brought to the world by the reckless devil-jackal son of
> un-mountable mother,

MARY: a boy must be made to look like a boy and a girl
> must be made to look like a girl and we must look like
> Nommo –

MRS: – no more!
> A duel of duals has ensued since then
> Repeated the world over
> In religions, traditions, medicine.

Justified
With knives,
Scalpels, razor blades and needles in hand
To make a woman a woman

MARY: and a man no less than a man…

MRS: This is an old tale of tails…

MARY: But, once we were two

MRS: When two was one

MARY: And some of us want to go home.

End animation.

DJ SON: Here's 'Bright Star', the Sunset Remix.

Track plays.

SCENE – WHY?

MRS: Why…?

MARY: Tradition.

MRS: Yes but why?
Tradition.
Later she said:

MARY: Mrs I asked my mum, about that thing.

MRS: Did you? What did she say?

MARY: She said English people don't understand and I should never talk about it. I'm not talking about it, okay, Mrs?

MRS: Okay.

MARY: She said it happened to my brother too, when he was thirteen, but I was younger and braver. I got bigger party, I got new dress and Elsa dolly from *Frozen,* you know, 'let it go, let it go…' Okay I am too old but still everybody happy, everybody give us money – much more than my brother!

MRS: That's different Mary, what they cut off the boys ain't the same.

MARY: It's not true. My mum said, little girls have a bit, little boys have a bit, both gets cut, because if we didn't, boys grow into girls and girls grow into boys and no one knows who is who.

MRS: It don't grow into a willy, Mary…

MARY: *(Upset.)* And then I ask why they close me, why I cannot pee, why it hurt so much Mum…? *(Recovering.)* She says it happen to her too, and to my grandmother and to every lady body I know in my family since the beginning of time. She say it make us clean and calm. Pure and perfect girl for marriage.

MRS: Mary, it's not right.

MARY: But my mum said!

MRS: Mary, what you got, what you *had*, down there, no one is supposed to touch unless you want them to, and when they do it is supposed to feel…

MARY: It's supposed to feel…?

MRS: Nice.

MARY: Nice? *(I.e. is that all?)*

MRS: *(Realising the inadequacy of 'nice'.)* Like the best thing in the whole world!

MARY: What is the best thing in the whole world?

MRS: I dunno. Ice cream. It's supposed to feel like ice cream in the summer down there. It won't make much difference to your brother, Mary, except he'll probably never get his winkle caught in his zipper.

MARY: I don't understand.

MRS: Neither do I.

MARY: It is supposed to feel nice? It just hurts…

Pause.

You feel nice? With Mr?

MRS: You can't ask me that!

MARY: Why you ask me questions then?! I am not a girl anymore Mrs. I know things now.

MRS: I don't feel nothing, he's dead.

MARY: No, before he went to heaven…? What was it like, on your wedding night?

MRS: He's not in heaven, Mary, there's not a hell big enough for him and it was never like ice cream. I only married him because I thought I had to after what happened in the fridge.

MARY: Fridge?

MRS: This ain't about me, Maryam. You and me dear, it is not the same.

MARY: Why?

MRS: Because you're just a child and I'm an old girl. I'm a soft old bourbon in the bottom of the biscuit tin. I've had my chance at happiness, you ain't!

MARY: I have happy chances, lots of them. You are making me sad! I am going be a spacewoman. Like Nommo! My mum and dad love me. They're not like you and Mr! This our culture. If I didn't get cut no husband would want me. And what will happen to me if no one will want me in this far-away country where no one says hello, how is your mother, father, sister, brother…? My family love me… It's just… Owwwwwwww… I have to pee.

MRS: She shoved past me and then left straight after that. *(MRS gets her vape. Smokes a little.)* Didn't stop for chocolate or a chat. Came back the next day but wouldn't cross my doorstep. Holds that doll from *Frozen* in a shiny green dress. Thrusts it in my face –

MARY: *(With doll.)* Look!

MRS: 'Let it go, let it go…' You coming in?

MARY: Underneath – LOOK!

MRS: What is it?

MARY: Nothing. Nothing there. Just like me. I am pretty.

MRS: You are pretty, Mary.

You need to pee? Come inside –

MARY: – NO! Mum says –

MRS playing MARY playing MARY'S MOTHER, suspicious, taking Maryam aside.

MARY'S MOTHER: Maryam, come. Why only *you* goes to her house? You know people in this country always doing funny funny things to children. I see it on TV every day. Maybe she is a paedo. Maybe she is a witch. Stay away from that old woman. Okay? Come here. *(Cuddles her daughter.)* Good girl.

MARY: Maybe I am cut but you are cut too, Mrs. Cut off and covered in scars. But I am going to the stars. I am going to be a space woman, the first woman from my country, and I don't need this dirty thing. My mother and my father they brought me here, they –

MARY'S FATHER: *(Stern but honest.)* – sacrificed everything and provide everything.

MARY: I don't need anything. And when I grow up I will provide them.

MRS: That's right. That's right. Look come inside and let's –

MARY: No, no, no! There is nothing for me inside. There is nothing for you! Just a cigarette that is not a cigarette, a cat that is really a fish, science that is fiction, *The Mirror* with no reflection – just made-up stars and a son who hides inside the radio to keep away from YOU! Sorry. Sorry. You should go outside Mrs, instead of watching it from the window. Mum says I am not allowed to come anymore.

MRS: And she starts to cry and she starts to pee and she shuffles away, across the estate.

What about your school project? Mary! Maryam! Your book! *(Waving the stars school project book which has been left behind.)*

She didn't look back.

I watched out from my window after school but I couldn't see her for days. So I done like she said. I go outside. *(Acting out the memory.)* Knock on their door. *(Pause.)* Nothing. Look through the letter box and…a black hole… Like they were never there. And ever since that night, I been having this recurring dream…

DJ SON: '3am'…from Bearcubs…

221

SCENE – ECLIPSE

Animation of the dream, with music and DJ SON's voice in voice-over, subtitles.

DJ SON: *(Voice-over.)* The cold moon passes in front of the sun.
   We all stand in the playground with cardboard glasses on.
   All the neighbours look up at the sky,
   But you are looking at the neighbours,
   Searching the crowd, for her.
   Some cry, some cheer, some shiver with fear.
   The birds fall silent,
   And we all feel bitterly cold.
   It starts to rain
   And when we go back up to the flat,
   The door is open,
   The radio is white noise,
   And the fish is floating in the bowl…
   And you know…
   You *know*…
   (Quoting the film Blade Runner.*)*
   'All those moments will be lost in time.
   Like tears in rain.
   Time to die…'

End animation/voice-over.

MARY: Gravity is a grave,

MRS: she'd say…

MARY: It can only go one way… No matter how hard we pray…

MRS: I couldn't go back to mass after that. I had no stomach for praying to a virgin. I had no stomach for tradition, religion. I had no stomach for any of it. I want to leave this flat, this planet. *(MRS gets her phone, music shifts to 'Elegant and Never Tiring' by Lorenzo Senny.)* I phone my Mikey in the middle of the night, crying, 'I've had enough, "beam me up", I wanna go to the stars, with Mary.' He thought I meant that euthanasia clinic in Switzerland. *(Crying, distraught.)* 'No, no you don't understand, Mary came to me, Mary revealed it all, and she made me think about everything I've denied in my life and then she just disappeared as if she was never there, as if she was just a story in *The Mirror* and then last night I had a dream about an eclipse and I heard your voice and now I think she might be dead and she was my sun, my son, she was my reason for getting up in the morning. Michael, Michael *listen*: at the centre of the whole constellation, there's a bright little girl, there's no future without her but no one can stand to face her… We close our eyes. This is your mother, "signing off, signing off…"' And he thought, 'Alzheimer's.' *(Beat.)* That brought him home for Christmas. *(DJ SON comes down from his studio to sit with MRS.)* Got cover for his radio show and bought me – *(MRS unwraps the gift from DJ SON, delighted.)* – an 'iPad'! Spends Boxing Day teaching me how to use it.

DJ SON: You can look up your stars. Even does crosswords.

MRS: Ohhh… And do you think I can send one of them 'e-mails' on this?

DJ SON: It's a whole universe in there, Mum.

MRS: Our first Mr-less Christmas. Watched old clips from *Star Trek*!

Now I can apply for that Spexit. *(Quoting her horoscope.)*
'The start of a personal adventure.' That's what my stars said.

DJ SON: Live long and prosper, Mum.

DJ SON returns to his radio studio.

MRS: Mary will be up there! Betcha!

DJ SON: That was 'Elegant and Never Tiring' by Lorenzo
Senni... Time to 'Chase the Devil. *(After the lyrics 'Lucifer
son of the morning, I'm gonna chase you out of Earth!' DJ SON
says...)* Lee 'Scratch' Perry.

SCENE – MRS' BIOGRAPHY

*MRS speaks during the opening dub section of the track. She searches
on her iPad.*

MRS: Project Spexit/*Virgin* Space Travel Programme.
Application. *(Like Richard Branson.)* 'So, first off, tell us a
bit about yourself...'

*Listens to music, rocking, smoking her vape, thinking about what
to write on the application. She speaks after Lee Scratch Perry's
lyrics, 'I'm gonna put on a iron shirt and chase Satan out of earth,
I'm gonna put on an iron shirt and chase the devil out of earth,
I'm gonna send him to outer space, to find another race, I'm gonna
send him to outer space, to find another race...' Track switches to
dub version from here.*

MRS: During the war I was born, 1944
Throwaway baby of a runaway English wife and a black
American G.I.
But a Jamaican mum and Irish dad rescue me
From a children's home.
Black and white Catholics doing the Lambeth Walk
Mum and Dad were the talk of Southwark.

They always wanted a baby
And didn't mind the controversy.
I was two when they got me
And me mum said I was frozen,
Staring off into space
Whatever they did to me in that place it was no home.

But eventually I learnt to look at adults again
Dreamt of becoming our school's first brown nun,
I could never imagine growing up to marry a man
And that was all that was expected of you back then.
I loved needlework and I was good at Latin,
Weren't I qualified?

But Mum said –

MRS' MUM: *(Jamaican, gentle.)* Why on Earth you want to be a
nun – be a nurse like me, that's close enough.

MRS: But Dad said –

MRS' DAD: *(Irish, soft.)* Sure we need money coming in if
we're ever gonna build that house in the Blue Mountains.

MRS: So just before I'm due to start nursing training
Dad gets me a summer job in the sandwich factory

MRS: Where he drives deliveries with his drinking buddy,

MRS' DAD: That joker, Terry.

MRS: I'm appointed as 'top filling mixer'.
No production line for me
And packaged sandwiches were the future
In 1960.

She gets up, steps into her memory.

Then one hot day, it's egg mayonnaise

So I go into the big fridge
To collect a bucket of eggs
And in comes Terry.
Pulls the big fridge door shut
Says,

TERRY: *(White, cockney, Jack-the-Lad.)* Cwor it's hot. Wanna help me cool off?

Music changes to 'Mourn' by Corbin.

MRS: I'm frozen to the spot.
Could have been a nurse,
Could have been a nun.
Sixteen years young.
I come out staring into a bucket of eggs
Shivering, bleeding, can't feel me legs
Ashamed.
Two weeks late.
Pregnant.
So Terry asks Dad for me hand
Dad buys a bottle of whiskey
Mum kissed me
I sew a yellow dress
And up we all went down the registry office.
And since that day everybody just called me 'Mrs' Terry Manners.

MR: Mind your manners, Mrs!

MRS: He'd say.
'As long as you mind yours, Mr!'
I'd reply.
And he gets us this council flat all the way over in Woolwich –
(An aside.) Might as well have moved to fucking France.
He carries me across the threshold and I giggle.

MR: I hope my Mrs ain't frigid.

MRS: I never laugh at that particular crack.
    But I do learn to smile again,
    Even learn to like him,
    He was happy-go-lucky,
    Says:

MR: I could love you, if you let me.

MRS: Gives up deliveries and starts painting and decorating
    (Referring to the flat.)
    Getting everything ready for our new baby.
    Says he was

MR: a good man really.
    Not a lot of other white blokes would

MRS: want me.

MR: And we look good together, don't we?
    Milk and tea,
    our baby will be the sugar.
    You should take it nice and easy…

MRS: But our baby was born as still as a Sunday morning
    And from that day
    Terry never stops drinking
    And I never stop thinking about Gabrielle
    My angel,
    And what she could have been,
    And what she was doing now,
    Above the clouds with Jesus…

    Never did do that nursing training…
    My dear old mum nursed me until
    I went back to work at the sandwich factory

And all the girls gave me fags and made me sweet tea
'So, so, sorry…'
I hardly let Terry touch me after that
I only had to look at him and he froze.
I'd stay up late to avoid it
Watch the box
(An aside.) Any old shit…
Years went by with Terry down the pub
And me sitting on the sofa,
Stroking the cats and staring at the sci-fis on the silver screen…

And then one day the Evangelicals come knocking at the door

CHURCH ELDER 1: Come to a Sunday Celebration?

MRS: Thought, why not, what am I stuck in here for?
And I finally got pregnant with Michael
And Mr finally left me alone.
Years of affairs but I didn't care.
Got meself a nice desk job at British Telecom –
'Hailing frequencies open, Captain'.
Life was the girls at BT, my son and science fiction.
No worries, no plans, no expectations…
But when Michael left home I was stricken with grief again.
Couldn't get up for work anymore and they packed me in.
I was due for retiring…

SCENE – SHELLEY

DJ SON plays Jonzon Crew's version of 'Space is the Place'.

MRS: I know.
There's something missing.

Forgive me father for I have sinned
It's been years since my last confession.

1984:

Before the Evangelicals came to my door, before Michael
was born...

I never imagined anyone could want me,

Love me,

Make love to me...

Until one day

A lady in a laundrette offers me fabric softener with

Two drops of her own pressed lavender

And a smile that says –

*SHELLEY is a musician from Lancashire, rich accent, nomad, free
spirit, laid back.*

SHELLEY: I handle delicates with care.

MRS: And somewhere between slow soak and fast spin
Everything feels washable and new.

(In the laundrette now.) The laundrette was my sanctuary,
That's one place Mr would never follow me.
The men who did come in with their black bin bags
Always looked a little found out

SHELLEY: Huddled over their smalls
Hoping no one sees their white streaks and brown skids,
Ashamed of their own fluids...

MRS: Shelley was as easy as her name and the Lancashire rain.
She saw me watching her and asks –

SHELLEY: Want a bit?

MRS: Oh, sorry for staring I just...

SHELLEY: Wondered if it makes a difference?
It does, it really does.

MRS: And that's how it starts.

SHELLEY: Have some lavender for your smalls.

MRS: Oh no, it's my husband's jumpers and me cat blankets!

SHELLEY: Aw shame, well let's make them all the fluffier
shall we…?

MRS: We'd mostly meet on my morning off, a Monday…
Oh hello Shelley, how are you?

SHELLEY: Shattered.

MRS: She'd been singing at some festival or other
While I spent the weekend smiling at spillages on his shirts
Throwing bras in the yellow basket without a care in the world.
She said she finds

SHELLEY: the laundrette relaxing. Watching the washing go
round and round.

MRS: Earth turning around the sun.

SHELLEY: And the heat is better than the new leisure centre
sauna and you didn't have to deal with all the men asking
about your tattoos.

MRS: Shelley's got a lot of tattoos and piercings, purple
streaks and a couple of teeth missing.
She looks like a pirate, and just as brave
And I only got one invitation.
She wanted to show me her van.

SHELLEY: Correction: classic converted UPS delivery truck.
Pine cabin inside – I did it all up meself.

MRS: And I turned no more than ninety degrees before she
kissed me,
Unfolded me

And stretched me out, like a clean sheet.
And I couldn't believe this was happening to me,
'Life begins at forty'.

There was so much water…
I never knew there could be so much water…
Like she was the force conducting the tides
And not the moon,
Not the moon at all…
And she rowed across my belly
(Acting out all of this.)
Like a pirate on the sea
She smuggled me.
I looked up from the deep
And on and on blindly
She crossed the ocean
Swelling inside me
Until she reached her island in the sun
And arched her back
And threw back her head
And sang out a YESSSSSSSSSS!
And crashed like waves upon my chest
Sshhhhhhhelley…
So that is what it is like,
I'd seen it in films but…
That is what it's like,
When it's real,
It is *so powerful.*
No wonder they keep trying to stop women from having them.
And me, I was just terrified of what it might do to me,
That if I exploded like her supernova
I'd never be able to put meself back together!

SHELLEY: Come on Mrs, your turn.

MRS: No. Shelley. Just, hold me.
    And she did. Gently. And I wanted nothing more.

SHELLEY: Correction: you don't feel you *deserve* anything
    more. You need to go home tonight, lock the bathroom
    door, light some candles and have a hot bath with
    lavender oil, lay back, let it all go and love yourself first
    Mrs. No one else has a chance unless you do.

MRS: I'll give it a try…

SHELLEY: *(Quoting* Star Wars.*)* 'Try not. Do, or do not.'

MRS: *(Finishing the quote, their little joke.)* 'There is no try.'
    Bye. *(Kisses SHELLEY goodbye.)*
    But I went home to Mr instead
    And said:
    'It's time we got a washing machine.'
    And I weren't being mean.
    I just knew it was all over as soon as it began
    Because when I looked up at her she was closing her eyes
    and mine were open wide.

    Hail Mary, Full of Grace
    The Lord is with thee
    Blessed art thee amongst women…

    Mondays especially I'd miss her
    So instead of the laundrette I'd visit the convent and sit
    with the old nuns
    (Momentarily sitting with the nuns in the convent.)
    And wonder if they'd ever had one,
    And wonder what my life could have been
    If I had a nun's habit instead of a smoking one,

And been married to gentle Jesus instead of Mr Terry
Manners.
Who died on the toilet,
Cradling an empty bottle of whiskey,
Like a baby.

MRS' action conveys the end of the online application.

DJ SON: Here's another one of mine, a remix of Jamila
Woods, 'Way Up'…

SHELLEY/MARYAM'S SONG

*SHELLEY sings an a cappella version of 'Way Up' by Jamila Woods at
one of her gigs. MARY reappears singing and also in animation.*

SHELLEY: I'm an alien from inner space
(Lyrics continue until:)
I'm ready to run
And rocket to sun
I'm way up
I'm way up[2]

*From here MARY/MARYAM is singing, and animation is projected
of her going into space.*

DJ SON: Going back up with Sun Ra…

SCENE – MRS DOES THE CROSSWORD

*Time has passed. MRS wears her glasses, does the crossword, listens to
music, smokes her vape (a cloud of smoke) writes/searches on the iPad.*

MRS: Seven down
'Nerve ending of female pleasure. The Latin for shame'.

---

2   Lyrics and music by Jamila Woods, https://www.youtube.com/
watch?v=fGVW5T7R2U0. Accessed 11/06/18.

P space space E space space space.

Looks on the iPad for the answer, scanning her findings, reflected in the animation.

'As big as a phallus, on the inside:
The clitoris.
Twice as sensitive as the head of a penis
The only organ in the entire human body
Designed purely and only
For pleasure.'
I been Googling.

MRS Googles 'cutting clitoris' on the iPad. She follows a film on YouTube.

'Two hundred million women and girls all over the world
Clipped, cut, sliced, sewn up,
Some left only with a hole the width of a matchstick
And on their wedding night, the groom takes a knife and…'
YouTube.

Overwhelmed. Resumes crossword.

Seven down
P space space E space space space.
'The nerve ending of female pleasure'
(Thinks.) 'Pudenda'
'The Latin for shame'.

MRS suddenly thinks she hears MARY in the toilet. Switches off the radio. No music. Silence for the only moment in the play.

MRS: Mary?
Maryam you in there…?
You out there…?

Silence. MRS, a little afraid, turns on the radio again to fill the space.

MRS: Eclipse, significance:

    'Secrets, omens… Hidden emotions…'

    'Something missing'

    'Turmoil, repressed'

    'Fear of failure,

    Fear of success'.

    Eclipse, science:

    'A cosmic coincidence'.

    What are the chances?

    That I'd get invited to lunch, by Maxi.

DJ SON: 'Sunday Morning' by Seven Davies Junior…

SCENE – MAXI

MRS: Maxi was younger than me, we used to work at BT.

    We'd have such a laugh back then, but I retired and we drifted apart.

    But recently Maxi got married to my butcher, Barry.

    He's always decent to me.

    Extra chipolatas since Mr died.

    Started to feel there was a little bit of hope.

    Company and cut-price pork chops,

    They live above the shop.

    One January Saturday when they were closing up,

    Maxi invites me up for Sunday lunch.

    MAXI is in her fifties and young with it, black, bold, full of life, power and joy.

MAXI: Barry will be off dangling his maggots in the canal and I can't be bothered to do a roast just for meself. Come up and see me.

MRS: I bought a nice bottle of wine and a box of Quality Streets.

We chatted for hours.

Maxi said Barry the butcher was good to her.

The women are tipsy.

MAXI: I got him trained! Now he's a damn good lover!

MRS: I confided in Maxi on the sofa:

I took no pleasure in Mr whatsoever

He might as well have been rubbing sandpaper

He paid more attention to cutting in and decorating than he ever did to me.

MAXI: Poor you. Me and Barry lift off every Saturday night after *Britain's Got Talent!*

MRS: I knew. Everybody knew. You could hear it halfway up the high street.

MAXI: It's cos of my SUPERPOWER!

MRS: Your what?

MAXI: Shall I tell you a story?

MRS: Go on then.

MAXI: You sitting comfortable? When I was born, a Doctor, named Money, stood at the end of my mother's hospital bed and said: *(MAXI plays DR MONEY, upper-class, cold, arrogant, English surgeon.)*

DR MONEY: I'm afraid your 'daughter' has ambiguous genitalia. But we'll perform simple surgery, a quick clitoridectomy to cosmetically correct the clit–

MAXI'S MUM: *(Who is from Jamaica.)* – but wait!

DR MONEY: It is far too big to be a normal clitoris.

MAXI'S MUM: Says who?

DR MONEY: Professors Prader and Quigley!

MAXI'S MUM: Well if I had given birth to a son who was hung like a donkey would we still be having this conversation Dr Money? No, I don't think so.

MAXI: And you know what he said?

DR MONEY: It is deformed! If *that* was hanging off of your face you'd have a job…

MAXI: You'd have job?!

MAXI, outraged, goes off on one, fast, rapping along to the music.

A nose job
A facelift
A tummy tuck
A cellulite suck
A botox pump
A breast implant
Buttock enhancement
Wax
Sack back and crack
Bumhole bleach
Designer vagina
Vagina tightener
Labia reduction
Hymen restoration
Circumcision
Snip-excision
Clitoridectomy
Infibulation
Any old genital mutilation
On or off the NHS
What's the difference?!

Beat. Back to the scene with MAXI'S MUM. DR MONEY on the attack.

DR MONEY: Do you want her to have an abnormal life? How will she ever get a husband, be a *normal* wife – this child will grow up confused!

MAXI'S MUM: Rewind, rewind, selector, come again…
(DJ SON rewinds the vinyl.)
Let me get this straight…
You wanna take my baby,
Guess what them would have looked like,
If them didn't look like what them do
Make them look like something that them don't
So it easier for you to know what box to tick on what form?[3]
I think you is the one that's confused Dr Money!
You can change the boxes on that form in your hand,
But you nah change my baby.
Put your scalpel back in your pocket.
The Lord makes no mistake!
I shall call her: 'Maxi'.
And if she favour a boy, she can call himself Maxi same way. No problem.

MAXI: *(As herself.)* They call me 'intersex' and I say too right I am into-sex! Heheyyyy!
I'm a Black Panther!
I got a bigger superpower than the King of Wakanda!
(Doing the 'Wakanda' greeting, larger than life now.)
You can keep your vibranium!
I don't need no vibrator!
My body is natural and my orgasms are out of this wooooooooooooooorld STAR!!!

---

3 Paraphrased from an interview with Jim Costich, in *Intersexion*, dir. Grant Lahood, 2011 accessed at https://www.youtube.com/watch?v=QQdOp3COfSs 01/06/18.

DJ SON plays 'Cosmic Slop' by Funkadelic. Pause to take it all in.

MRS: Wow… Inter-sex…

MAXI: There's millions of us all over the planet. It's as common as being a redhead, but it's not connected, otherwise nuff Irish people would be hermaphrodites innit? *(Laughs gently to herself at the thought.)* Seriously though, you never really know what's going with people inside, or down below. And I am one of the lucky ones. Cos most intersexys be much worse off than me. I read all about it in *TO THIS DAY!* Magazine. Operating on people with no permission! Doctors lying to us, hiding us, humiliating us, shaming us. Secret surgeries, making out we got cancer, forcing us to be one way or another. Worldwide! It's a *(quoting)* 'Gendercide!'[4] Doctors ain't supposed to play God, doctors ain't supposed to lie! Doctors ain't supposed to decide which bits of my privates look right to their eye! And get this, when I was eleven yeah, the doctors wanted to operate on me AGAIN, but my mum says –

MAXI'S MUM: They been messing with black women bodies since slavery days!
Chain and bit, speculum and whip. Anyone try touch you and we'll sue!

MAXI: And I got the balls to do it! Two, still on the inside doing just fine. Yes!

MRS: Bloody hell Maxi, you never said…

MAXI: No one talked about it back in the day. But I found this online action group. First off Barry didn't want me to get involved. Didn't want everyone knowing. I said: *(To*

---

4 Intersex activist Hida Viloria and others termed the phrase, 'gendercide'. See https://hidaviloria.com/quoted-in-exc-washington-post-intersex-rights-movement-article/ accessed 22/02/19.

BARRY, really going for him.) I'm not exactly going on *Jeremy Kyle* or *Oprah*, Baz, it's only a website! But he says:

BARRY: *(Slow, kind, lumbering, cockney.)* Let's just keep our sex life 'tween you and me, we only just got married Maxi.

MAXI: It ain't about sex Barry, it's about – *(Precisely quoting something she has read.)* – 'bodily integrity'.[5]

BARRY: Eh?

MAXI: Anyway, he's come around now.

MRS: Has he?

MAXI: He's much more open-minded since I found him his G.

MRS: His what?

MAXI: His G spot. I found it.

MRS: Did you? Where?

MAXI: Up there. *(Simple gesture toward her bum.)*

MRS: *(Half-laugh half-scream in horror.)* No! No! No!

MAXI: *(Gleefully.)* Yes! Yes, yes, Mrs! Every man's got a G spot up his bum. Just most men are just too proud to let you at it, or too scared it might hurt, but when they do – woooooooooooh! *(Singing.)* 'Free your behind and your mind will follow!' It ain't me you can hear screaming down the high street Mrs, it's Barry hahahaa! He is so happy… *(MAXI is proud of herself.)*

MRS: Really, Barry, up his bum? I'll never be able to look at his chipolatas the same way again. *(Pause for thought.)* Why

---

5 Thank you to Intersex activist Valentino Vecchietti for this line and expert feedback on this scene. Thanks to Intersex activist Del LaGrace Volcano also.

the good Lord in his infinite wisdom chose to put a 'G spot' in a man's bumhole I will never know.

MAXI: Same reason he blessed us with a clitoris! You should count yourself lucky you got one! Have a holiday!

MRS: *(Drifting for a moment.)* Yeah… *(Snapping back.)* Can't be that much of a sin then, can it Maxi? Enjoying your…self.

MAXI: What you on about, Mrs? I never understood your thing for religion. Priests, rabbis, urologists, gynaecologists – they're all the same to me. They just wanna control you! They wanna cut off my beautiful big clit! But you wanna hear us on a Saturday night after *Britain's Got Talent! (Beat.)* This chicken's dry. You having that stuffing?

DJ SON: That was 'Cosmic Slop' by Funkadelic. And here's Lyman, taking us down 'Joy Road'…

MRS: As Maxi tucks into the remains of my plate I contemplate all it means for me…

MRS: My mind wanders to all the hours I spent with the Evangelicals… Trying not to sneeze… Praying for the missionaries smuggling Bibles into Communist China. I wondered if there were any ladies left in Beijing, toddling along on their tiny little feet, stumps, two inches wide. Men found their tangled toes attractive, apparently, even under rotting bandages. *(Exhaling in disgust, distress.)* I wondered if anyone in China ever prayed for me.

Pray for me…

MAXI: *(Who has been watching MRS.)* You all right old girl?

MRS: Sorry, where's my manners, I am forgetting myself. Whatchusay?

MAXI: You're drifting off a lot lately. You okay…?

MRS: I don't think so, Maxi. I don't think I am…

DJ SON: 'Perotation', Floating Points.

SCENE – THE GP

MRS: Me husband died
    And it's taken my whole life
    But Doctor,
    I've never had one
    And I want one
    Before I die…

    My orgasm has got to be out there
    Somewhere!
    I know you all think I'm losing it
    That I'm some kind of a…space cadet
    And you might just be right about that!

    So one last job for you, Doctor:
    I'll be needing a medical certificate
    To prove I am fit for travel.
    I'm going away.

SCENE – THE PLAN

MRS is hurriedly packing whilst reading from MARY's stars project book, as if it is an instruction manual. MRS' speech is directed at Cat. Fragments of animation drawn from the project book are projected as MRS is trying to piece together her plan. The animation could be fragments that we have seen throughout the play, running through the scene and then the climax at the end.

MRS: Cat, there is three things they don't tell you about space travel. One:

MARY reappears to MRS, spirit-like.

MARY: It is extremely painful.

MRS: Up there
   Your body is a blissful skin bag of sinews and bones
   Floating freeeeeee
   But when you land home
   The force
   Is like a car crash –
   I'm not talking whiplash
   I mean every part of you feels crushed
   And you can spend the rest of your life killing pain.

MARY: Gravity is a grave.
   No one is supposed to know.

MRS: Disabled astronauts ain't the poster NASA wants to sell ya!
   But that don't bother me…we're only able-bodied *temporarily*
   Cos the other thing they don't tell you about travelling to
   space is…
   When you're up there, the orgasms are out of this world!
   Hahahahahahaha…

   MRS hears Cat in her head – 'What?'

   I know Cat, that could be an 'alternative fact'
   But it is one I am prepared to believe
   Cos think about it
   Where else do all the orgasms go?
   All that energy!
   All that power!
   Must go somewhere?!
   'The Earth moved!'
   'I saw stars!' – 'Shooting stars!'
   Ain't that what people say?
   'Yes! Yes! Yes!'
   There's nothing down here for the likes of me and
   The likes of Mary…

(Remembering SHELLEY.) 'Love *yourself* first Mrs... There is no try.'

And Maxi's right an' all

I need a holiday!

One way.

A mission,

To have a 'petite mort' before I die!

To come and go!

Perhaps sometimes to climax you gotta go that far!

And I ain't bothered about the pain landing back cos I plan to stay in space.

I seen enough saucers flying past my head to last me a lifetime down here

Give me one last pleasure

For all my trauma,

Let me fly!!!

'Spexit'.

Sound of an e-mail pinging in an inbox. MRS is so excited!

THE REPLY!

Reading the email optimistically:

'Dear Mrs...

As you are only a second-generation immigrant of the Windrush Generation you are *not* eligible to apply for the government's 'Spexit': relocation space flight. Priority is given to migrants, asylum seekers and refugees from majority Muslim countries.'

Charming!

And to Trump it all, Richard Branson wouldn't have me either:

'We know this will come as a disappointment but the *Virgin* Space Travel Return Programme is only eligible for young people between the ages of eighteen and twenty-five.'

Pause. Disappointment. She smokes her vape.

MARY: You missed number three!

MRS looks in MARY's stars book again.

MRS: The third thing they don't tell you about space
travel is…

MARY: There is more technology in a modern-day washing
machine
than the Sputnik that took the rocket dog to heaven
all on his own in 1957.

MRS: HAIL MARY!
I got a washing machine
and a fridge!

*MRS finishes packing by putting the urn in the fridge. Entering a
trance-like state, wide eyes; music gets louder, building to the climax!*

One small step
For a woman.
I'll boldy go
To *inner* space.
I shall
Shut
My
Eyes.
Tight.
I'll take the Gs
Dare
To forget myself
And remember
Who I am![6]

---

6   Thank you to Sue Mayo for this line!

I will be afraid

No more. NO MORE!

My name is NORMA MONAGHAN but you can call me
NOMMO!

My name is Norma Monaghan and I am coming HOME
OHHHHHHH – YES!!!

MAY THE FORCE BE WITH *ME!*

MAY THE FORCE BE WITH YOU!

MAY THE FORCE BE WITH US AAAAAAAAALL!

MY SUN! MY SON! HAIL FREQUENCIES OPEN!

MRS shuts her eyes. Dances wildly, as if she is inside a fast washing machine cycle, until the end of the track which stops suddenly. Blackout. Breathing into the silence for three beats. DJ SON plays 'Scudd Books', the track from the opening. Mirror ball? Club night/ star lights.

DJ SON: But remember, this is just the beginning. See you
on the dance floor down at *(whichever theatre/venue we
are playing in)* 'til two a.m. Night's called *STARS* – a
celebration of pleasure. Open to all. Entry is free.

A community chorus of women technicians in jumpsuits burst on stage, transforming the space, collectively constructing the rocket. Alternatively the construction could combine projected animation and/or motion capture, with the help of the audience. The women dress MRS/NORMA MONAGHAN in the Nommo costume and mask from the opening. She takes the goldfish bowl, now a space helmet, and gets into the rocket. The concluding credits of the show are projected, animated in MARY/MARYAM's handwriting. The show transforms into a club night – a celebration of pleasure.

THE END